INTRODUCTION

In 1940 many of the world's nations were at war, their armies and navies supported by massive air arms, many of which were larger than the United States' then small but progressive Air Corps. That year the US Army Air Corps consisted of only 51,165 personnel and under 4,000 aircraft—though doubled over its strength of the previous year. This expansion had begun in 1939 when President Roosevelt requested Congress to fund a programme for an Air Corps of 10,000 planes. It seemed then an ambitious goal, but events would prove it a modest one.

Many tend to think of the American World War II air arm as the Army Air Corps, but this was not its wartime designation. What had been the Air Service was redesignated the Air Corps on 2 July 1926, a combatant arm of the Army. On 1 March 1935 the Army established the General Headquarters Air Force (GHQAF) to command Air Corps tactical units. GHQAF existed as a co-equal command with Chief of the Air Corps, both reporting directly to the Army Chief of Staff. Not until 1 March 1939 were these two organisations placed under the command of a new Chief, Army Air Corps. With the expansion of the air arm the GHQAF was removed from the jurisdiction of the Chief, Army Air Corps, on 19 November 1940 and given separate status under the commander of the Army Field Forces. It was not until 20 June 1941 that the Army's air organisations were consolidated under a single command, the Army Air Forces (AAF); the GHQAF became the Air Force Combat Command. The AAF was now one of the three major components of the US Army together with the Army Ground Forces and Army Service Forces. Though still a part of the Army, it had the status of a semi-autonomous service.

Upon America's entry into the war, the combined AAF comprised some 22,524 officers and aviation cadets, 274,579 enlisted men, and 10,329 aircraft. The expansion of the AAF was rapid and massive. It reached its peak strength of 2,372,292 in 1944; and a total of 230,287 aircraft were procured by the war's end, though some of these were provided to the Allies.

The AAF's contribution to the war effort was substantial. A total of 2,362,800 combat sorties were flown worldwide, in which better than two million tons of bombs were dropped. Over 40,000 enemy aircraft were destroyed in the air and on the ground, while millions of tons of shipping were sunk. Equally huge quantities of troops and cargo were transported. The armies on the ground may have finished the enemy and liberated the occupied nations, but they did so generally free from enemy air attack due to the AAF and the other Allied air forces.

The cost was grim. With more officers than any other Army branch, the AAF's combat losses among officers was higher, over 51,000 killed, evacuated because of wounds, missing, or captured. Only the infantry suffered more enlisted casualties than the AAF: almost 68,000 enlisted men died—a higher ratio than any other branch—another 15,000 personnel were killed and injured due to the demands of realistic training in the States. Overseas aircraft

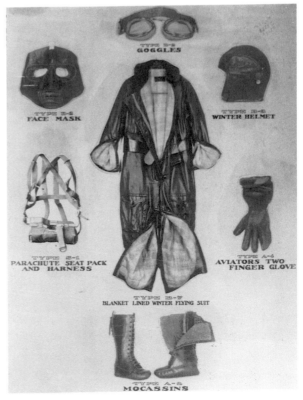

A display of late 1920s Air Corps winter flying clothes and equipment. All leather items were seal brown. B-7 leather, blanket-lined winter flying suit (centre) and, anti-clockwise from top: B-2 goggles, B-3 winter helmet, A-4 aviator's two-finger gloves, A-2 fur-lined moccasins, S-1 parachute seat pack and harness, and B-2 face mask.

losses totalled about 43,600—just over half from combat action, the others by mechanical failure, error, weather, or retirement because they were simply worn out or obsolete.

Books abound describing the AAF's impressive combat record and detailing the characteristics of the many aircraft; but little has been published to record what the men inside the machines wore to stay alive and effective in the air and on the ground, or, as often as not, in the water. This book will discuss the flying clothes, accessories and equipment worn and used by individual airmen fighting their often desperate battles in the sky.

The forthcoming *US Army Air Force 2* will discuss basic organisation, badges, organisational insignia, service uniforms and work clothing common to AAF personnel, plus unique insignia and uniforms worn by aviation mechanics, aviation cadets, Air Women's Army Corps (WAC), flight nurses, Women's Airforce Service Pilots (WASP), aviation engineers, AAF military police, Civil Air Patrol, air carrier contract personnel, civil flight instructors, and civilian technical representatives.

FLYING CLOTHES

While flying clothes might be considered a minor aspect of America's air war effort—especially in light of the AAF's massive expansion, the huge numbers of aircraft procured, and the worldwide scope of operations—this was not necessarily so. A major effort was expended in the development and procurement of flying clothes. The climatic extremes of worldwide theatres of operation were a problem encountered by all forces, but the aerial environment's brutal hostility to the human body in flight proved to be especially demanding. From the tropics to the arctic, in jungles and mountains, on shark-infested or freezing waters, airmen had to be provided with suitable clothing and protective gear permitting them not only to survive, but to function effectively. One flyer might need a flotation and exposure suit to survive a ditching in the North Atlantic, or he would die within minutes, while another might require suitable clothing and footwear to enable him to walk out of a rugged tropical or mountainous area. Neither one of these ensembles was suitable for use at high altitude due to the flyer's need for protection from the cold, freedom of movement, and comfort during long flights.

Bomber crews, as often portrayed in the movies wearing tailored service uniforms, leather jackets, 'fifty mission crush' caps with earphones, sunglasses, and unencumbered by oxygen masks, were clothed quite differently than those actually fighting swarming Messerschmitts at 25,000 ft. in −65°F (−84°C) temperatures, with the accompanying frozen oxygen masks, frostbite, and oxygen starvation, and burdened by heavy clothing, parachutes, and flak jackets.

Designing clothes to enable airmen to survive and function effectively in such a hostile environment proved no simple task. Many early items were flawed by designs that limited freedom of movement, were too bulky in confined spaces, or made of materials ineffective for protection in harsher than anticipated environments. Procurement was also plagued by contractor production problems, with start-up delays, lower quality materials than specified, inadequate manufacturing equipment, lack of materials meeting specifications, and unforeseen material shortages. This was compounded by the constant expansion of the AAF beyond any expectations, and a never-ending flood of complaints and recommendations from the clothing's

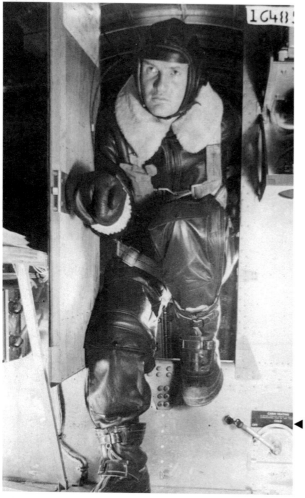

◄ *A 1944 airman demonstrates the bulkiness of shearling flying suits. He is wearing the winter AN-J-4 jacket and AN-T-35 trousers, AN-* *H-16 winter helmet, A-9 gloves, and A-6A shoes. The details of the A-6A's instep and top securing straps can be seen.*

US Army Air Force (1)

Gordon L Rottman · Illustrated by Francis Chin

Published in 1993 by
Osprey Publishing, Elms Court, Chapel Way, Botley,
Oxford OX2 9LP, United Kingdom.
Email: info@ospreypublishing.com

ISBN 1 85532 295 1

Series Editor: MARTIN WINDROW
Filmset in Great Britain by Tradespools Ltd, Frome,
Somerset
Printed in China through World Print Ltd.

FOR A CATALOGUE OF ALL BOOKS PUBLISHED BY
OSPREY MILITARY AND AVIATION PLEASE CONTACT:

The Marketing Manager, Osprey Direct UK,
PO Box 140, Wellingborough, Northants,
NN8 2FA, United Kingdom.
Email: info@ospreydirect.co.uk

The Marketing Manager, Osprey Direct USA,
c/o MBI Publishing, PO Box 1,
729 Prospect Avenue, Osceola, WI 54020, USA.
Email: info@ospreydirectusa.com

www.ospreypublishing.com

Acknowledgements

A special thanks goes to Michael V. Eckels of the
Arkansas Air Museum, Fayetteville, Ark.; the staff of
the US Air Force Historical Research Center,
Maxwell AFB, Ala.; Robert G. Borrell, Sr.; David A.
Neighbors; John S. Ross; Jim Thomas; Ron Volstad;
and Charles 'Red' Wilson. I wish also to thank my
wife, Enriqueta, for her assistance with the material
related terminology. All photographs are period
USAAF images.

Abbreviations

AAF	Army Air Forces
AF	Air Force (numbered or named)
AN	Army-Navy (standardisation programme)
GHQAF	General Headquarters Air Force
OD	Olive Drab
QAC	Quick Attachable Chest (parachute)
QMC	Quartermaster Corps
QRB	Quick Release Box (parachute harness fitting)
WASP	Women's Airforce Service Pilots

Artist's Note

Readers may care to note that the original paintings
from which the colour plates in this book were
prepared are available for private sale. All
reproduction copyright whatsoever is retained by the
Publishers. All enquiries to be addressed to:

Francis Chin
615 Cricket Court
Edmonton
Alberta
Canada T5T 2B2

The Publishers regret that they can enter into no
correspondence upon this matter.

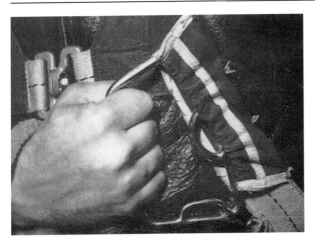

A close-up of a B-8 back parachute's ripcord handle and the older type of bayonet fastener on its chest strap. The 'crinkled' effect caused by the acrylic lacquer applied to this B-6 winter jacket led some airmen to call their shearling jacket a 'crusty'.

two commands, the Material and Air Service Commands, the former being responsible for flying clothes procurement. In the autumn of 1943 the Clothing Section became a branch, being separated from the Equipment Lab, and placed directly under the Material Command. In April 1944 the Personnel Equipment Lab was placed under the Command's Engineering Division and the Clothing Branch absorbed into it. A number of other agencies were also responsible to varying degrees for flying clothes development: Textile, Clothing and Leather Branch of the War Production Board; AAF Equipment Board, and Aero Medical Laboratory.

Prior to America's involvement in World War I, the Signal Corps purchased flyers' leather coats, sweaters, helmets, gloves, and mufflers from commercial sources. An Aviation Clothing Board was established in 1917 and the procurement of specially designed flying clothes was soon begun. Flying clothes was an entirely new field for the clothing industry, and ideas were borrowed from clothes used by explorers, trappers, motorcyclists, and Eskimos; all used fur and leather to retain body heat and provide protection from the wind.

The 1920s saw many new developments which were to influence the early World War II clothing in style and materials. The B-1 winter flying suit, adopted in 1921, was made of leather and lined with dog fur obtained from China. Its odour led to its nickname 'monkey suit', forcing its recall in 1931. One-piece leather winter flying suits, such as the blanket-lined B-7, shearling-lined B-10, and silk pile-lined B-9 and -11, were introduced in the late 1920s and early 1930s. The one-piece B-10 and B-11 suits were redesigned as two-piece suits, the B-1 jacket and A-1 trousers and B-2 jacket and A-2 trousers respectively. Both remained in use as limited standard until 1944. Their design was to influence the later shearling suits. The hip-length jackets and pocket-festooned, high-waisted trousers of World War II were a far cry from the romantic double-breasted, three-quarter-length leather coats and tailored

users and developmental agencies. The need for protective flying clothes was so crucial that it was found during the winter of 1943/44 that the number of UK-based AAF bombers available for combat missions was determined more by the amount of adequate crew clothing available than any other factor.

The details of flying clothing pattern, style, fit, comfort, and ease of movement presented many problems. Military regulations and requirements had to be met in pattern and colour, and the number of types procured needed to be kept to a minimum. When suits were designed, the question of whether to use one or two pieces; ease of donning and removal; cutting to fit sitting positions; size ranges; degree of protection; position and number of openings; use of zippers; number, position, size and shape of pockets; availability of materials and qualified manufacturers, and more, all had to be taken into consideration, along with integration with goggles, oxygen, survival and radio equipment.

Since 1919 the development of flying clothes was the responsibility of the Equipment Section at McCook Field, Ohio. It was moved to nearby Wright Field in 1926 and placed under the new Material Division, where it was redesignated the Equipment Branch (later designated Laboratory), and included a Clothing Section. In 1941 the AAF's various logistical functions were consolidated under

The A-1 and A-2 jackets, both made of unlined leather. The buttoned A-1 was of olive green calfskin with dark green wool knit collar, waistband, and wristlets. The A-2 was seal brown horsehide with dark brown knit collar, waistband, and wristlets.

Officers assigned to Operation 'Carpetbagger', mid-1944 clandestine airlift missions into France to supply the resistance. The two to the left wear A-2 jackets; the centre and extreme right men, light OD winter combat jackets (issued to armour troops), and the second man from the right a 'Parsons' M1941 field jacket (issued to ground troops). They stand before a Waco CG-4A Hadrian glider.

riding breeches favoured by aviators in the Great War.

Conflicting interests and overlapping activities of the Air Corps and Army Quartermaster Corps (QMC) also caused problems with the procurement of flying clothes. The QMC was actively engaged in the development of cold climate clothes and equipment in 1941, but there was no attempt by the Air Corps to avail itself of the accumulated data and experiences. Early in the war QMC clothing was sometimes preferred by airmen over AAF issue. The QMC maintained that it should have full control over the development and distribution of personal clothing and equipment for all branches of the Army. The AAF contended that its relatively small size (flying personnel then made up less than 3% of the entire Army) and unique requirements demanded special attention in research, development, production, and distribution. Flying clothes development remained in the AAF's hands but, subsequently, closer contact with the QMC was affected.

Non-AAF aviators, e.g. spotter/liaison aircraft pilots assigned to field artillery and tank destroyer units, used some of these same flying clothes.

Nomenclature

AAF flying clothes were under Supply Class 13: flying clothing, parachutes, equipment, and supplies not supplied by the QMC. Most items were designated by a letter system identifying the type within particular categories. The type letter was followed by a sequential number, usually in the order of standardisation. This might be followed by an 'A' to designate an improved version.

A particular item of clothing's nomenclature also included its description in the usual quartermaster's reversed jargon, e.g. 'helmet, flying, winter, type A-6'. In this book nomenclatures will be simplified and type dropped to conserve space, e.g. 'A-6 winter flying helmet'. Exact nomenclature for a given item often varied slightly between different AAF publications, however. To add to the confusion when attempting to identify surviving items, their identification tags are crowded with other numbers. An A-6 flying helmet's tag might include its military specification number—94-3126; a part number—42G6431-3 (large size); and stock number—8300-439060. All Class 13 stock numbers began with '8300-', the code number; the rest was the item's serial number, which also served to identify its size if appropriate. To add further to the confusion, mil. spec. numbers followed a wide range of systems, though most clothing items began with '94-', but some items had no spec. or part numbers. All this, plus a contract number. . . .

Clothing items were also designated as 'standard'—the most satisfactory available and preferred for issue; 'substitute standard'—usable substitutes for standard items to supplement shortages; or 'limited standard'—those items that no longer met requirements or were not as effective as standard items, but were suitable for use to meet supply demands. Newly standardised items were given the same stock number as the item they replaced if they had the same type number, e.g. B-3 and B-3A summer gloves. A unit requisitioning summer gloves might receive either type.

The type letters identified only broad categories of flying clothes, usually with no apparent pattern; there were many exceptions. Type A *usually* designated summer jackets (with no matching trousers), trousers (with matching type B jackets), summer suits, summer helmets, winter gloves, most footwear, and many other categories. Type B generally identified winter and intermediate jackets (with matching type A trousers), winter suits, winter helmets, summer gloves, and most caps. Type C identified early electric heated items; D, some mechanic's clothes; E and F, later electric heated items; G, anti-G suits; K and L, late war light flying suits.

In 1942-43 some items were designated under the Army-Navy standardisation programme and identified by an 'AN' prefix followed by a four-digit drawing number. However, they were more commonly known by their spec. number: 'AN-' followed by a category letter (H- Helmet, J- Jacket, S- Suit, T- Trousers) and a one- or two-digit sequence number.

Materials

To meet the wide range of flyers' environments, both climatic and high altitude, several materials were available from which to fabricate clothes and accessories. Cold protection was the most serious of concerns. At the beginning of the US bombing campaign in Europe in 1942, 70% of all combat casualties were caused by frostbite. Improvements in clothing and other protective measures decreased this to 20% by the end of 1943.

Fur-lined flying clothes were widely used into the early 1930s to include muskrat and calf skin complete with the hair. Nutria fur (a beaver-like South American rodent) was also tried. Wool blanket lining was used with suits made of corduroy and Bedford cloth. In 1934, in an effort to find warmer linings, both reindeer and sheep shearling were tested. Though both provided similar warmth, the latter was chosen as it could be made more uniform in thickness and shearling was a well-developed industry in the US. Furthermore, in the event of war, reindeer skins might be difficult to obtain; they had an objectionable odour, and shed their hair with age.

Sheep shearling is a pliable tanned leather retaining short-cut wool fleece on the inside. Several thicknesses of fleece were used: Type I—$\frac{3}{8}$ in. and $\frac{5}{8}$ in.; Type II—$\frac{3}{4}$ in. and $1\frac{1}{4}$ in.; Type III $\frac{1}{4}$ in. The pelts of young sheep were used, called 'electrified lamb skin' by the clothing industry referring to the manner in which they were dispatched. Their smooth appearance was obtained by alternately combing and ironing the wool after oiling; it was then clipped to the desired length and dyed beige. The wool fibres were worn inside the garment with the leather hide on the outside. Shearling hide, and virtually all other leath-

◄ *The 1941 light OD A-4 summer suit worn with a khaki A-8 summer helmet, A-2 jacket, and Stateside issue service shoes (smooth side out, capped toes).*

▼

The crew of an Antisubmarine Command radar-equipped B-18A bomber checks its planned patrol route. They wear *khaki AN-S-31 summer suits over khaki service uniforms. Three of the crew wear the B-1 summer cap.*

The 1944 khaki AN-S-31 summer suit is worn with a khaki AN-H-15 summer helmet, B-8 goggle, B-3 summer gloves, and stateside issue service shoes.

A P-47 pilot of the 360th Fighter Squadron wears an A-2 jacket over a greasy khaki AN-S-31 summer suit. He has added a celluloid-windowed map pocket and a flare pocket to the thighs; both pockets are dark OD. Two 37 mm M11 red, two-star flare cartridges are held in the flare pocket; they were used with the AN-M8 pistol and M9 projector.

discard the heavy garments on long treks and, if ditched in water, they were hazardous due to excessive weight. Efforts were made to render the leather more pliable and less water absorbent, but these failed—as did attempts to moth-proof shearling, which only led to the chemicals used causing more damage to the pelts than the moth. The fleece was also easily soiled by grease and dirt, and equally difficult to clean without damage. However, with the Air Corps' flying clothes programme in full motion, no serious effort was made to find a replacement material until after the war began.

In 1941 the AAF forecast the need for 16,000,000 sq. ft. of shearling in 1942 and 12,000,000 sq. ft. in 1943, 'excluding possible expansion during 1943'. This 'possible expansion' came not in 1943, but in 1942. It was determined that 87,160,000 sq. ft. of shearling was needed by the AAF alone; 75 sq. ft. were required for a single suit. The government undertook a programme to encourage sheep raisers to triple their production of pelts to 9,000,000 in 1943. None the less, it was recommended that the number of types of flying clothes be reduced, that multi-layer garments be designed, and that the development of more suitable flying clothes using other materials be expedited. This led to concern among sheep raisers, tanners, dealers, and packers that they would suffer financially due to their patriotic response to increase production. The development of new materials continued, and the government met its moral obligation to the shearling industry by purchasing all stocks; the Department of Agriculture then took measures to decelerate shearling production. No additional shearling purchases were made after 1943, though shearling garment production continued into 1944. By late 1944 all early types of shearling garments had been withdrawn from overseas service (though shearling jackets were retained by many flyers) and only the final version was still in use, and then only in the United States.

The replacement material chosen was alpaca: a medium grey, wool-like rayon, double-faced ($\frac{1}{4}$ in fibres on both sides, though early alpaca was $\frac{1}{2}$ in. single-faced) material backed by wool fabric and made in imitation of alpaca hair—a Peruvian animal similar to a llama. Alpaca-lined garments had a water-repellent cotton boat cloth shell. Mouton—dark brown dyed sheared sheepskin—was used in some garments as a collar facing or hood lining. In May 1943 the AAF Equipment Board recommended that flying clothes be made of these materials, along with down-filled extreme cold weather garments. The Army Service Command directed in August 1943 that the use of shearling cease and all flying clothes production for 1944 be made from the new materials.

Chamois, an extremely soft and pliant leather prepared from sheepskin, was used to line some flying helmets. In

ers, were 'seal brown'—a very dark brown, almost black. These garments had leather binding and trim. The leather of many shearling garments was coated with a dark brown polyacrylate dye and then lacquered making it oil-, gasoline-, and water-resistant. As these garments aged the lacquer coating developed a fine pattern of cracks and sometimes peeled off giving it a crust-like appearance, causing some flyers to refer to their jacket as a 'crusty'.

The standardisation of shearling and the design of the first garments were rushed due to an immediate need for suitable flying clothes, since the Air Corps was going to assume responsibility for flying the Air Mail[1], which demanded long-range, cold-weather flying. It was not long before complaints began to emerge describing shearling garments as too heavy, inflexible, and cumbersome. While warm and windproof, the material did not permit the escape of perspiration. If downed, flyers were often forced to

[1] The Air Corps assumed responsibility for the Air Mail on Presidential Order, due to private contractor problems, on 19 February 1934. Since the Corps was neither trained nor equipped for the mission it was a dismal failure, and the Air Corps terminated the service on 1 June.

1943 doeskin, made from the pelts of South African or Brazilian sheep, replaced chamois helmet lining as it was more uniform in thickness. Horsehide was also used in unlined components; and use was also made of goatskin, pony hide, and capeskin (a light pliable leather made from sheepskin). Besides seal brown, some leather items were 'russet', a reddish brown. Most of the soft leathers used for lining were natural tan. Wool cloth, knitted worsted wool, and wool/rayon blends were also used as lining and garment components.

Use was also made of down-filled, quilted, satin-lined winter garments. Some winter garment outer shells and summer suits used wool/cotton blend gabardine. Water-repellent, tightly woven cotton twill boat cloth was used as an outer shell for alpaca-lined flying clothes. Lightweight cotton Byrd cloth, an extremely tight weave (known as Grenfell cloth in Britain), was used in some summer suits; wider use was not made of this excellent fabric due to its expense. Summer suits were also made of cotton twills and mercerised cotton, a very light, lustrous fabric. Rayon, the first widely used synthetic fabric, was extensively used as garment lining.

Generally, cotton twill, gabardine, and Byrd cloth garments were khaki (tan or sand-coloured). Heavier cloth garments were usually light olive drab (OD). From 1942/43 most cloth garments were dark OD, a dark brownish green, the green being much more pronounced. OD shades varied greatly depending on period, fabric, and manufacturer. After repeated laundering, OD items generally faded to a grey-green.

Metal fittings (snaps, rivets, eyelets, etc.) were usually enamelled black, brown or green. Some larger fittings, such as buckles, were usually unpainted, polished metal. Plastic buttons and buckles came into wide use early in the war. On khaki garments these were tan or light brown, while on OD clothing they were dark brown or dark green. Zippers (or officially, 'slide fasteners') were made of brass, though other materials were tested, but all were jammed by corrosion.

The AAF subdivided flying clothes into several categories determined by weight and the temperature zones they were intended for. Very light suits were intended for the tropics, while light suits were for low-altitude summer flying. Intermediate suits were suitable for moderately cold conditions. Heavy suits were intended for winter and high-altitude flying. Electric heated suits, depending on the outer suits with which they were worn, protected the flyer in the intermediate to extreme cold at high altitudes.

Light clothes

In warm/hot climates air crewmen normally wore standard service or work clothing augmented by specialised gar-

This 1944 fighter pilot wears the khaki AN-S-31 summer suit, AN-H-15 summer helmet, B-7 goggles, B-2 summer gloves, and the experimental E-2 light combat, or 'escape', shoes styled after European designs.

ments, though the suits were often worn over only underwear in very hot climates. The flying jackets discussed in this section had no matching trousers, normally being worn with summer service uniforms or summer flying suits.

The **A-1 flying jacket**, later influencing the famous A-2 and Navy G-1 jackets, was made of olive green dyed lambskin. It had two small buttoned, flapped midriff pockets. The front opening was secured by buttons as zippers were not developed until 1928. The collar, wristlets, and waistband were dark green knitted wool. Its development began in 1923, but was not standardised until 7 November 1927. Although made limited standard on 9 May 1931, they saw limited use early in the war by those still possessing them. Remaining stocks were issued until declared obsolete on 29 September 1944. So far as is known, no surviving A-1 jackets are found in private collections or museums.

The **A-2 flying jacket** was an extremely popular item habitually worn as an outer garment, even when not flying; airmen never quite accepted that it was not a component of

The light OD gabardine L-1 light suit was a more modern design than its predecessors. The K-1 very light suit was of an identical design, but made of khaki Byrd cloth. On the left thigh is a brown leather-covered map clip. He wears an AN-H-15 summer helmet.

the service uniform! Its development had begun in late 1930 and was standardised on 9 May 1931. It was made of seal brown horsehide with dark brown knitted wool wristlets and waistband. It was originally lined with brown silk; later issues had tan and other coloured cotton or rayon lining. The 'Flying Tigers' used bright red silk lining if they had achieved ace status. It had a stand-and-fall leather collar with snaps beneath the points to hold them in place, and snap-closed, flapped midriff pockets. Of the many types of flying jackets the A-2 was the only one with shoulder straps. Cloth and hand-painted unit insignia often adorned A-2 jackets, along with usually gaudy, hand-painted artwork on the back similar to aircraft 'nose art'. Although made limited standard on 27 April 1943 and replaced by the almost identical **AN-J-3 (AN6552) flying jacket**, the A-2 remained in use until after the US Air Force was formed in 1947[1].

Several OD commercial design jackets, similar in style to the A-2, were issued as low-cost substitutes for the A-2. They were used principally by aviation cadets. The **A-3 and A-4 flying jackets** were made limited standard on 20 August 1940. Both were made of whipcord (a tightly woven, ribbed, worsted wool fabric). The A-3 was wool-lined and the A-4 unlined. They were less satisfactory than leather in appearance, durability, and ease of cleaning. Existing stocks were exhausted at the end of 1942. The **A-5 flying jacket** was adopted in mid-1941 and had a twill shell with a detachable wool-backed twill lining. The **A-6 flying jacket** was made of lightweight, cloth-lined whip-

[1] The A-2 jacket, with slight modifications, was reintroduced in about 1980.

cord. The wool-lined twill **A-7 flying jacket** had an elastic waistband and cuffs. Stocks of the A-5, -6, and -7 were exhausted in July 1943.

Prior to 1929 flyers wore standard QMC-issued, Air Corps summer service uniforms, with the appropriate accessories, in warm/hot weather. Beginning in 1929, several types of one-piece summer flying suits were adopted, all with integral cloth waist belts, neck-to-crotch front zippers, and chest, leg front, and shin pockets, among others. The summer designation is somewhat misleading in that some were made of comparatively heavy windproof fabric (even in the summer it can be fairly cool at lower altitudes), though some later suits were made of very light materials for use in the tropics.

The **A-3 summer flying suit** was made of light OD mercerised cotton with pockets on both chests and shins. The pockets, front opening, and ankle cuffs were secured by buttons. Standardised in 1928, it was made limited standard 18 March 1930, but issued until declared obsolete on 21 March 1944. The **A-4 summer flying suit**, standardised on 18 March 1930, was made of dark OD wool/cotton gabardine with a snap-closed collar. The sleeve and ankle cuffs were fitted with zippers permitting easy donning and removal. Zipper-closed patch pockets were provided on the right chest and right shin, along with internal front leg pockets. Due to complaints that it was too warm, from 1941 this suit was made of light mercerised cotton. It was made limited standard on 23 April 1943. A slate blue version of the A-4, the **A-5 summer flying suit**, was standardised on 23 June 1937. It saw very limited use and was made limited standard on 10 October 1941.

On 23 April 1943 the **AN-S-31 (AN6550) summer flying suit** was standardised to replace the A-4. Made of khaki cotton/wool gabardine with a stand-and-fall collar, it had buttoned, flapped pockets on both shins and chests (some only on the left chest), with internal front thigh pockets. Buttoned leg cuff closures and a zippered fly were added to the crotch seam in later versions. The lighter weight khaki Byrd cloth **AN-S-3 summer flying suit** was adopted for use in the tropics. The later **AN-S-3/A summer flying suit** was made of even lighter weight cotton poplin.

On 3 November 1944 two improved light suits were standardised and the AN-S-3/-3A and AN-S-31 were made limited standard. The **K-1 very light flying suit** was made of khaki Byrd cloth; it was developed from the A-6 summer suit standardised, but not procured. The **L-1 light flying suit** was of a heavier, dark OD cotton gabardine. These suits had larger pockets, zippered leg cuff closures for adjustments, ventilated armpits, and vertical zippered ventilation openings above the knees; they offered greater freedom of movement, and a brown leather

First Lieut. Robert L. Hite, a B-25B Special Project (cover name for the raid's composite squadron) pilot captured during Doolittle's daring 18 April 1942 raid on Japan, is led from a transport by MPs in Tokyo. He wears a B-3 winter jacket and OD service uniform. Three of the eight captured raiders were executed.

▼
Two pre-war designed seal brown shearling winter flying jackets: B-3 (left) and B-6 (right). Both were used well into the war.

covered spring-clip on the left front thigh for holding a map. The **K-1A very light** and **L-1A light flying suits** of early 1945 had modified cuffs and belts and the front zipper replaced by snaps.

The **A-9 summer flying suit** was adopted in early 1944 as a heavier weight suit. Made of dark OD cotton herringbone twill, it had internal front leg pockets and patch pockets on the chest, the right with a flap and the left without. The sleeve and leg cuffs were button-adjusted.

Intermediate and heavy suits

These suits consisted of a jacket and matching trousers. All jackets had front opening zippers while the more heavy duty models also possessed overlapping buttoned fronts. Most had at least two waist pockets. The high-waisted trousers had either zippered or buttoned flies and integral adjustable suspenders. All models had shin pockets and most had a third pocket on the left front thigh for the bail-out oxygen bottle. Most had knee- or full-length zippered outer seam openings to allow the donning and removal of the trousers while wearing boots. This was especially important to a ditched airman, as water-saturated wool shearling or alpaca would drag a man under; it also allowed some access to wounds.

The **winter flying B-3 jacket** and **A-3 trousers** were standardised on 8 May 1934 and issued the next year. Development was rushed due to the need for winter clothing when the Air Corps took over the Air Mail Service. It was also issued to ground mechanics until 1940 when they received their own type of shearling suit. The jacket is often referred to as the 'B-3 bomber jacket' under the mistaken assumption that the 'B' represented bomber as it did in aircraft designations. Influenced by commercial flying suits known as 'Alaskan suits', they were made of lacquered oil, gasoline, and water-resistant seal brown shearling. Originally the pile was ⅝in. thick, but in mid-1935 the jacket's pile thickness was increased to 1¼ in. in the torso and ¾ in. for the sleeves. The jacket had a zippered front with the opening, skirt edge, and cuffs trimmed with thick fleece. The very large fleece-faced collar could be secured around the neck by two brown leather buckled straps. On the right waist was an angled patch pocket. Adjusting straps and buckles were fitted to the sides of the longer than normal

The B-17F crew of 'Rosie's Riveters', 418th Bombardment Squadron, display a variety of clothing. Most wear A-2 jackets, but three wear the B-6. The second standing man from the right is wearing his wings above his hand-painted name, 'Bill'.

skirt edges. The A-3 trousers had a zippered crotch and full-length waist-to-cuff zippers on both legs. Non-flapped patch pockets were on both shins. The waist and cuffs were fleece trimmed. This suit was much criticised from the outset, for being too heavy and cumbersome, but it remained in use well into the war. They were made limited standard in mid-May 1943. The B-3 was declared obsolete on 29 September 1944, but the A-3 remained in use until after the war.

The **B-4 winter flying jacket** was standardised on 7 November 1935 as an arctic parka for use by both airmen and ground mechanics. It was not accompanied by matching trousers, the A-3 trousers being worn with it. It was made limited standard on 29 April 1941 and declared obsolete on 27 March 1944.

The **B-5 winter flying jacket** and **A-4 trousers** were standardised on 11 July 1938 as an intermediate ensemble for aircraft with enclosed cabins. It was made of light OD wool cloth and unlined, but had a shearling-faced collar. Except for materials, they were of the same design as the B-6/A-5 described below. They were made limited standard on 15 June 1939. For the remainder of the war they were mostly issued to flying cadets until declared obsolete on 17 March 1944.

A lighter and less cumbersome suit for use in milder conditions than the B-3/A-3 combination resulted in the **winter flying B-6 jacket** and **A-5 trousers** made of lighter weight seal brown ¼ in. shearling; in fact, actually an intermediate suit. Standardised on 12 June 1939, these proved to be satisfactory in the increasingly common enclosed aircraft of the day, but not for very cold or high altitude conditions. The jacket's collar, cuffs, and waist skirt were trimmed with fleece. The collar could be folded down

or secured around the neck with a strap and buckle. There were internal slash pockets at the waist. The trousers were of the same basic design as the A-3 including the full-length leg zippers, except that both shin pockets were zipper-closed and internal. They were made limited standard in mid-May 1943.

The **winter flying B-7 jacket** and **A-6 trousers** were developed in 1940 and standardised on 12 June 1941. They were intended for arctic conditions and made of natural tan 1¼ in. shearling; sleeves were ⅝ in. The hip-length jacket had a zippered and buttoned front, the buttons fastened to braided cotton cord loops. The front opening, cuffs, and skirt hem were trimmed with fleece while the integral hood's face opening was edged with wolf fur. There were internal zippered pockets at the waist and large non-flapped, brown leather patch pockets on the skirts. The A-6 trousers had a zippered crotch and full-length zippers on the outer leg seams. The cuffs were secured by zippers. Large non-flapped, brown leather patch pockets were on the thighs. This suit was made limited standard on 17 August 1942. In January 1943 the **winter flying B-8 jacket** and **A-7 trousers** were standardised for use as an inner liner with the B-7/A-6. They were made of an OD knitted wool pile fabric.

Development of the **winter flying B-9 jacket** and **A-8 trousers** began in September 1942. During testing the suit proved to be extremely lightweight, flexible, permeable to perspiration, and warm due to its down-filled, quilted satin lining. Intended for far northern operations in a temperature range of 14°F to –22°F, it was standardised on 22 July 1943. The light OD wool gabardine jacket's integral hood was lined and edged with dark brown mouton. Its front opening was secured by a zipper and large plastic buttons.

Internal flapped pockets were provided on the hip-length skirt along with opening slits for access to uniform pockets. The trousers were made of light OD cotton twill with internal buttoned flap pockets on the left thigh, both shins, and both hips. The cuffs were secured by buttons. Production suits proved to be a disappointment, however. Due to the armed forces' huge procurement of down-filled sleeping bags it was impossible to obtain the 100% eider down used in the test suits. Issue suits were 40% down and 60% feathers, which limited freedom of movement and made them heavier. Though feathers had the advantage of allowing the wearer to float for long periods (they were sometimes called 'buoyancy' or 'flotation' suits), this was of no real benefit as a man in arctic waters would survive only 30-40 minutes. Production was halted and they were made limited standard on 16 October 1944.

The **winter flying AN-J-4 (AN6553) jacket** and **AN-T-35 (AN6554) trousers** were the last of the shearling garments and incorporated the most functional aspects of earlier suits. They were standardised in mid-May 1943 to replace the B-3/A-3. The jacket, with ¾ in. shearling in the torso and ¼ in. in the sleeves, had a zippered front with a large fleece-faced collar fastened by a throat tab. The cuffs were fitted with internal wool knit wristlets. There were buttoned, flapped patch pockets on the waist. The ¼ in. shearling trousers had a zippered fly and double-acting zippers on the outer leg seams running from waist to cuff. Button-secured, flapped pockets were provided on the left thigh and both shins. Unlike those of earlier trousers, the

suspenders were very wide in order to bear the trousers' weight more comfortably. By late 1944 it was the only shearling suit still being issued, but was used only in the States. It remained standard until made limited standard in late 1945.

The development of the **intermediate flying B-10 jacket** and **A-9 trousers** began in October 1942 and they were standardised on 22 July 1943, along with the decision to replace shearling. They were made of light or dark OD boat cloth, lined with wool-backed ½ in. single-faced alpaca pile. The jacket had a zippered front. Its dark brown mouton-lined collar could be folded down or secured around the neck with a strap and button. There were buttoned, flapped patch pockets on the midriff and a large, inside chest pocket. The wristlets and waist band were made of dark brown knitted wool, dark OD on later versions. Some early ones were fitted with shoulder straps. The A-9 trousers had a buttoned fly and cuff closures. Buttoned, internal, flapped pockets were provided on the left thigh, both shins, and hips. Opening slits permitted access to uniform pockets worn under it and also allowed the electric heated suit cord to pass through. Designed to provide protection down to 15°F, the B-10/A-9 could also be worn

The alpaca-lined ▶
intermediate B-10 jacket and A-9 trousers with A-11 intermediate helmet, red lensed B-8 goggles, A-6 winter shoes, and A-11 winter gloves. This late version of the jacket has dark OD knit wristlets and waist band rather than dark brown.

▼

(Left): The natural tan shearling B-7 winter jacket intended for arctic use, with hood ruff of wolf fur.

(Right): The OD B-9 winter jacket had a down-filled, quilted satin lining and brown mouton-lined hood.

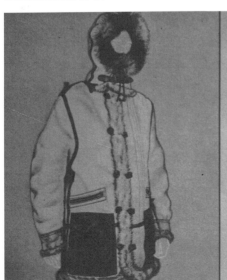

over the F-2 electric suit in much lower temperatures. It was also used by fighter pilots without the electric suit. The suit was made substitute standard on 7 April 1944 with the introduction of the B-15/A-11 suit, and limited standard on 7 February 1944.

The **winter flying B-11 jacket** and **A-10 trousers** were almost identical to the disappointing B-9/A-8 in design and materials, which they subsequently replaced, but were lined with wool-backed ½ in. single-face alpaca pile fabric rather than down-filled, quilted satin. The lower trouser legs were lined with wool fabric only. The B-11 jacket's hood was lined and edged with dark brown mouton like the B-9's. The jacket had an internal elastic belt, and the neck opening and jacket and trousers cuffs had adjusting tabs. When worn over an intermediate suit such as the B-10/A-9, it provided protection in the same range as the B-9/A-8 suit. This ensemble was especially useful to airmen in aircraft not fitted with electric suit outlets or

requiring only limited movement. They were standardised on 22 July 1943.

While satisfactory, the B-11/A-10 suit had room for improvement and the **intermediate flying B-15 jacket** and **A-11 trousers** were standardised on 7 April 1944 to replace their predecessors and, eventually, all shearling suits. Based on the B-11/A-10, they included a number of improvements including a more roomy cut for increased freedom of movement. Wool-backed, double-faced ½ in. alpaca pile now lined the garments. The dark OD boat cloth jacket had a full-colour AAF insignia printed on the left shoulder. Its wool knit wristlets and waist band were dark OD. The dark brown mouton-faced collar was larger and secured by a mouton-lined tab. On its chest were non-flapped, angled, internal slash pockets; there was a pencil pocket on the left upper sleeve, and a large inside chest pocket. The trousers had internal, snap-secured, flapped front thigh and shin pockets on both legs plus a bail-out bottle pocket on the left upper thigh. Full-length zippered openings were installed on the outer seams. These were fitted with a quick-exit feature. They were made limited standard on 4 November 1944.

Additional refinements were made on the **intermediate flying B-15A jacket** and **A-11A trousers** standardised on 4 November 1944. These included small triangular, brown leather tabs on the jacket's left and right chest on which to clip an oxygen hose, radio cord retaining strap on the left lower torso, a square bellows pocket on the left thigh to contain the bail-out oxygen bottle's hose, and the bail-out bottle's leg pocket was moved up 3 in. to prevent a knee injury during parachute landing. These suits were intended for a temperature range of 14°F to 50°F and were also worn over the F-3/F-3A electric suits. They were made limited standard on 21 May 1945, the same date the **intermediate flying B-15B jacket** and **A-11B trousers** were standardised. Its major modification was a rayon lining for cleanliness and easier donning.

The most important aspect of the alpaca-lined suits was that they were developed in conjunction with new electric heated suits. Used in combination, or separately, they provided adequate protection from the cold, increased freedom of movement, and were comparatively light in weight.

A B-17 radio operator in 1944 wears the winter AN-J-4 jacket and AN-T-35 trousers, the last of the shearling suits. He is also outfitted with AN-H-16 winter helmet, A-9 gloves, and A-6A shoes. On the right vertical chest strap of his A-2 QAC parachute harness (chest pack is detached) is a parachute first aid kit. He is drinking from a Tappan B-2 food warmer cup; one of the warmer's trays rests on his work table.

SPECIAL PURPOSE SUITS

Electric heated suits

The Army Air Arm developed its first crude electric heated flight suit in 1918. Some further development work was conducted in the 1920s, but no serious attention was given the subject until 1940, though the unsatisfactory C-1 electric heated flying suit was standardised in 1938. The increased pace of long-range, high-altitude bomber development was responsible for the renewed interest. The programme faced a number of difficulties including inadequate materials, particularly wiring; unreliable temperature controls; and insufficient aircraft power output. Another problem was that damaged wires had caused injuries to the wearer in earlier suits. Opponents argued that in the event of a suit malfunction, aircraft electrical failure, or bailout, the airman would lack sufficient protection from the cold—a justifiable concern. Within some units in 1943, up to 75% of the frostbite cases were caused by electric garments failures.

Regardless of these concerns, the General Electric Co. developed suits for service testing in mid-1940. These were standardised on 4 April 1941 as the **E-1** and **F-1 electric heated flying suits**. It was not until June, however, that modification orders were issued to install power outlets in bombers, both operational and in production. These were one-piece coverall-type garments worn under standard two-piece winter flying suits to protect aviators from the extreme cold at high altitudes. Electric heated gloves and shoes (described below) were components of these suits. Both suits were identical except for two aspects, the E-1 was used in aircraft with a 12-volt battery system (B-24, B-25, B-26) and was light grey ('Bunny Rabbit' suit). The F-1 was used with the B-17's 24-volt system and was light blue ('Blue Bunny'). The front was closed by a neck-to-crotch zipper and crotch-to-ankle zippers on both legs. A small zippered opening was located to the right of the crotch for natural relief; former airmen have stated that this was simply accomplished without opening the zipper due to the extreme cold—and no, there was no danger of electrocution! Electrical heating wires were sewn into the suit's wool fabric, basically the same as a commercial electric blanket. The electrical cord junction box, fitted with an ambient control switch, was on the right waist with a 2 ft. power cord (later suits had this same cord); all suit types were also supplied with a 6 ft. extension cord. Electrical connectors for the heated gloves and shoes were fitted above the wrists and ankles. Black knitted wool wristlets and anklets were fitted, as well as a similar collar. The wir-

An unrestricted view of the winter AN-J-4 jacket and AN-T-35 trousers with an A-11 intermediate helmet, A-8 goggles, A-10R oxygen mask, A-11 winter gloves, and A-6 winter shoes.

ing used could not withstand repeated flexings, and considerable trouble with breakages was experienced. They were wired in series, and a single break would cause the entire suit, gloves, and shoes to cease functioning.

The number of suits that a given aircraft's power system could support dictated how many the crew could use. In B-17s the priority went to tail and ball turret gunners due to their static, cramped duties; if the aircraft's generators could produce ample power, the waist gunners would also wear the suits. In B-24s they were worn by the waist and tail gunners. Some airmen wore the electric suit over several sets of long underwear, or a wool uniform and underwear rather than the prescribed single set of long underwear. This much extra clothing served in practice to insulate the wearer from the suit's heat resulting in cold injuries. The need to wear the suit over only underwear caused another problem, however: if an airman was downed over enemy territory, he did not have suitable clothing for evasion, or more realistically, in which to spend the duration in a *Stalag Luft*. There were also sizing problems with the E-1 and F-1 suits, and this, coupled with the bulky shearling suits, made movement even more awkward.

Development of improved suits continued into 1943. Suitable wire, able to withstand better than 250,000 flexings, was not developed until May 1943. The new suit was designed in conjunction with the alpaca B-10/A-9 suit, which could be worn over the electric suit as could shear-

This B-17 bombardier wears the down-filled winter B-9 jacket and A-8 trousers. This light OD suit's hood is trimmed with brown mouton. He also wears A-12 arctic gloves and A-6A winter shoes. He carries a light OD duck E-1 bombardier's information file containing computers, watches, bombing tables, plotting devices, penlight, pencils, etc. Similar brown leather satchels were also used for mission orders, maps, weather data, and signal instructions.

ling suits; or it could be worn under light flying suits. The 24 volt **F-2 electric heated flying suit** was standardised on 13 August 1943. It was a four-piece ensemble comprising electric heated jacket and trousers inserts and unheated outer jacket and trousers. The inserts were made of light OD wool blanket material incorporating more flexible wiring and wired in parallel, eliminating the failure problem with breakages. Electrical controls and fittings were similarly placed as on the E-1 and F-1 suits. Without current

the suit was comfortable down to 32°F, and with current, down to –30°F. It was better fitting and allowed greater freedom of movement than earlier suits. The wool-lined dark OD gabardine outer jacket and trousers, with suspenders, were of a simple design with a zippered front and flapped chest pockets; there were no leg pockets or leg seam zippers. An electric connection was fitted in the right chest pocket to plug in a B-8 goggle or oxygen mask heater. Some had a shearling-lined collar. It was designed to be worn over long underwear, wool service shirt and trousers. For additional protection, a light flying suit could be worn over the outer suit. It was made substitute standard on 19 February 1944 when the **F-2A electric heated flying suit** was standardised with thermostats to control the heat.

In the winter of 1942/43 there was a shortage of electric suits in England. An investigation showed that large numbers of E-1 and F-1 suits had been purchased, but most were still stored in stateside depots; issue was pushed and procurement of the F-2 rushed. To make up shortages, British electric gloves and boots were modified to allow their use in US aircraft[1]. Though an improvement, the F-2 suit was far from ideal, still not providing the needed freedom of movement.

Development of the **F-3 electric heated flying suit** began in late 1943 and was standardised on 19 February 1944. This well-designed suit was a two-piece style consisting of a dark OD cotton and rayon twill jacket and bib type trousers. It was designed specifically to be worn over long underwear, wool service shirt and trousers, and under the A-15/B-11 suit. As such, the ensemble provided complete comfort at –60°F, though even a light flying suit could be worn over it in 'milder' climates. In the event of suit or power failure or bail-out, the combination provided sufficient protection for a considerable time, and also allowed for suitable clothing for ground wear. The waist-length jacket was a collarless design with elastic cuffs and closed by a zipper. An auxiliary power connector was fitted on the left chest for connecting heated goggles, and a 'pigtail' connected the jacket and trousers circuits. The trousers had a high bib front, covering the chest, and fabric suspenders. Double-acting, full-length zippers were fitted to the outer seams. Electrical controls and fittings were greatly improved, as was the parallel wiring system, which permitted half the heat to still be supplied if one of the two circuits failed. Snap fasteners connected the gloves and boots to the power circuit. The outfit was better fitting and accommodated more individual size variations by mixing the two pieces. The F-3 was made limited standard on 21 October 1944 when replaced by the **F-3A electric heated flying suit**. It featured even more improved electrical controls, fittings, and wiring.

[1] For additional information on RAF flying clothes, see MAA 225, *The Royal Air Force 1939–45*.

Anti-G suits

Serious research in countering the effects of centrifugal force during high-speed, violent manoeuvres by fighters began in 1942. High G-forces (2–3 Gs were common) during inside loops or pulling out of a dive forces blood toward the lower part of the body; this leaves the brain without sufficient oxygen, resulting in, first grey-out dimmed vision, followed by black-out and unconsciousness. During outside loops or termination of a dive, the opposite occurs and blood rushes to the head resulting in red-out—red vision, eye pain, and a throbbing head. Pilots learned to level off gradually from dives and climbs and would tense their muscles and yell in an attempt to counter the adverse effects, but this had only marginal counter-effects. G-forces also increase fatigue.

Early attempts to develop an anti-G suit were ineffective. Finally, at the end of 1943, a development called the gradient pressure suit (GPS) looked promising. Encased in the suit was a series of interconnected rubber bladders positioned over critical portions of the legs and abdomen; the bladders were automatically inflated when a vacuum instrument pump, integral to the fighter's air pressure system, sensed 1.5 Gs. An air hose emerged from the suits' left side to connect with the metering valve to the left of the pilot's seat.

The GPS type **G-1 fighter pilot's pneumatic suit**, developed by the US Navy, was procured in very small numbers. It was a bulky set of two-layered, chest-high overalls made of light OD, inelastic, lieno-weave cloth. It had four bladders over each thigh and calf plus one over the abdomen, this latter held in a separate corset-like belt reinforced with seven steel stays. The 17 bladders were inflated with a complex triple pressure system. The suit's excessive 10 lb. weight was supported by suspenders. There were zippers on the sides of the abdominal belt and two more running the suit's length. Adjustments (the suit had to be snug fitting) were accomplished by laces on the legs, thighs, and flanks plus internal leg adjustment straps. The suit was heavy, difficult to don and remove, restrictive, uncomfortable, hot, and complex; it was seen that a change was necessary.

The G-1 was quickly followed by the **G-2 fighter pilot's pneumatic suit** using a much simplified single pressure system. It was similar in outward appearance to the G-1, but had long rectangular bladders, one over each calf and thigh, plus the abdominal bladder—a total of only five. The new design also eliminated much of the G-1's rubber tubing and reduced its weight to 4½ lbs. Standardised on 19 June 1944, they were issued to Eighth and Ninth Air Force fighter units in Europe. However, a still further simplified, cooler, and lighter suit was desired.

The development of the G-2's replacement began in January 1944. Two types were developed in parallel, using a much simplified bladder system comprising five air cells positioned in the same manner as the G-2's. The **G-3 fighter pilot's pneumatic suit** was actually a skeletonised set of high-waisted 'trousers' made of two layers of dark OD nylon; its crotch, hip, and knee areas were cut away. Fitting was accomplished by adjusting a lacing system; once fitted, it was removed and donned using leg-length zippers. Pockets were fitted to both shins. It could be worn under a flying suit and over underwear or over a uniform and under the flying suit; the lacing would have to be readjusted if clothing worn under the suit was changed, due to the need for a very snug fit. There were two variants of the G-3. The 2¼ lb. David Clark Co. G-3 had a single-piece gum rubber bladder system with a rubber tube crossing the small of the back extending 2 ft. from the suit's side. The 2¾ lb. Berger Brothers Co. G-3 used a vinylite-coated nylon cloth bladder system and had its air tube running across the abdomen. The tube was encased in a nylon sleeve and extended one foot. These early suits were issued as requested by the theatres of operation air forces. The Clark G-3 was standardised on 10 March 1945.

The G-3's final production version was the **G-3A fighter pilot's pneumatic suit** based on the Clark G-3 suit with an improved neoprene bladder system and other minor refinements, though it weighed 3¼ lb. The G-3A was issued to all fighter pilots without special requests being required as with the G-3. It was standardised on 10 March 1945.

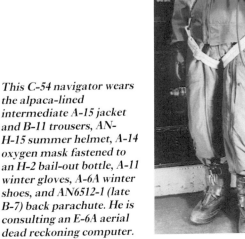

This C-54 navigator wears the alpaca-lined intermediate A-15 jacket and B-11 trousers, AN-H-15 summer helmet, A-14 oxygen mask fastened to an H-2 bail-out bottle, A-11 winter gloves, A-6A winter shoes, and AN6512-1 (late B-7) back parachute. He is consulting an E-6A aerial dead reckoning computer.

◄
Another view of the intermediate A-15 jacket and B-11 trousers with A-11 intermediate helmet, A-14 oxygen mask fastened to an H-2 bail-out bottle (its green cable-release is visible), A-11 winter gloves, A-6 winter shoes, and B-4 life vest.

A bomber crewman ▶ *demonstrates the burden of full equipment: intermediate A-15 jacket and B-11 trousers, A-11 intermediate helmet, A-14 oxygen mask attached to an H-2 bail-out bottle, B-8 goggles, A-11 winter gloves, A-6A winter shoes, C-1 emergency vest (M1911A1 pistol under left arm), B-4 life vest, and A-4 QAC parachute harness (chest pack is detached).*

After all the effort to perfect the anti-G suit, they were little use in practice. By the time they were issued in large numbers, their requirement had evaporated as there were virtually no enemy fighters left in the sky, so that there was little need for high G-force generating violent manoeuvres.

Flotation and exposure suits

Several types of flotation and exposure suits were developed prior to the war; all lacked sufficient protection and were too heavy and bulky. The need for adequate exposure suits was greatly emphasised by the increased flying over the North Atlantic and Aleutian Island areas early in the war. A requirement existed for an exposure suit capable of sustaining life in water temperature of 65° to 35°F.

One of the earlier suits still in use at the outbreak of war was the **C-2 flotation suit**. It was a one-piece OD coverall with foam flotation pads in the chest and collar. While providing flotation, its use of standard flying helmets, gloves, and shoes did not adequately protect the wearer from cold water. It was standardised on 23 October 1928 and used until declared obsolete on 13 March 1944.

On 29 January 1945 the completely sealed, buoyant **R-1 quick-donning anti-exposure flying suit** was standardised. This was a one-piece coverall made of orange-yellow two-layer neoprene-coated nylon with integral hood and boots. F-1 exposure gloves were contained in the large, snap-closed, flapped, bellows leg pockets (see Gloves section). The suit was issued in a pull-tab opened, 6×12×12 in. container made of the same material as the

suit. One was provided to each crewman/passenger in all bombers and transports flying overwater routes. It was also part of some life-rafts' component equipment. The suit was large enough to fit all individuals and intended to be donned over standard flying clothes and helmets, necessary for sufficient insulation. It offered protection down to 28 degrees F. Its fullness also provided flotation although it was recommended that the life vest be worn over it.

HEADGEAR

A wide range of flying helmets were available to meet various special and environmental needs. They were intended to provide only environmental and noise protection, unlike today's high-impact plastic helmets offering crash protection. Most types consisted of a close-fitting headpiece covering approximately the wearer's hairline, but with ear flaps extending at least down to the jaw line. A leather chin strap, pierced with eyelets, was fixed to the right ear flap and secured to the left by a buckle. All had three snap fastened goggle keepers on the sides and back, a small adjusting strap above the nape of the neck, and hooked retaining straps to accommodate radio/intercom headsets. Those helmets with integral earphones had black rubber earphone retaining cups, kapok ring pads, and ANB-H-1 earphones.

Integration with the standard HS-18, -33, and -38 headsets, goggles, and oxygen masks was more seriously taken into consideration from 1943 and mask studs were fitted to all helmets from mid-1943. After August 1943 all new masks were fitted with studs to accommodate the A-13 and A-15 masks. Masks manufactured earlier were modified with fittings provided in the type Z-1 oxygen mask maintenance kit.

The **A-6 summer flying helmet** was made in both khaki and light OD cotton twill with a silk lining. Standardised on 13 March 1931, it was declared obsolete on 24 March 1944. The intermediate **A-7 summer flying helmet** was made of chamois-lined horsehide; standardised 3 May 1933, limited standard 24 March 1941, obsolete 29 September 1944. The **A-8 summer flying helmet** was made of wool-lined khaki gabardine. It was standardised 12 October 1933 and declared obsolete 29 September 1944 after limited use. These all had a chin strap with a plastic or leather chin cup. The lightweight **A-9 summer flying helmet** was made of unlined light OD gabardine, but with shearling ear pads, was cut slightly higher at the nape of the neck than other helmets and had a throat strap. It was standardised on 24 December 1941.

The **AN-H-15 summer flying helmet** was similar to the A-9 which it was to replace, but made of khaki Byrd cloth. It was developed under the Army-Navy standardisation programme incorporating many improvements and intended to replace all existing types, though earlier helmets did remain in use. It had a doeskin-lined leather chin strap and large earphone retaining cups providing improved noise protection. It was standardised on 23 April 1943.

The **A-11 intermediate flying helmet** was standardised on 6 August 1943 and made of chamois- or doeskin-lined horsehide, later sheepskin. Its ear flaps had circular headset cutouts and, unlike other helmets, extended beneath the chin, overlapped, and fastened with a small strap. It also had a turn-down brow flap. Large improved earphone retaining cups were integral to the A-11. Although intended for 14 to 50°F, it was found to offer protection down to −22° and was extensively used in all temperature ranges.

The AN-H-15 helmet was replaced by the **A-10A summer flying helmet** in early 1945, though the former continued to be used. It was of virtually identical design and materials, but had a chamois-lined brow flap (which the little-used A-10 lacked), velveteen padded chin strap, oxygen mask studs, and other minor changes enabling more efficient interface with accessories. The A-10A was a modification of the limited procurement A-10 of April 1944.

The **B-5 winter flying helmet** was standardised on 2 May 1933 and saw some use until declared obsolete on 29 September 1944. Made of ¼ in. shearling covered with horsehide, it had a leather chin strap and cup. The **B-6 winter flying helmet** was of similar design, but had a

Already having donned the jacket and trousers inserts of the F-3 electric suit, an airman consults his equipment checklist. The F-1 electric felt shoe inserts are connected to the suit's circuit. Hanging in the locker are the intermediate B-10 jacket and A-9 trousers. On the chair are F-2 electric gloves, AN-H-16 winter helmet, and A-14 mask with an H-2 bail-out bottle attached. Under the door is a pair of F-2 electric felt shoes.

turn-down shearling brow flap for extra protection and a drawstring for adjustment around the face and neck. It was standardised on 15 December 1941 and made limited standard on 23 April 1943 when replaced by the AN-H-16.

Two limited procurement helmets were the **B-7** and **B-8 winter flying helmets**. The B-7 was made of ¼ in. shearling with a wolfskin facepiece. It was procured for use in extreme cold and standard only from August 1942 to March 1944. The B-8 was a B-6 modified for a different type of earphone cup. It was issued briefly in 1944.

The **AN-H-16 winter flying helmet** was similar to the B-6 helmet in general design and made of ¼ in. shearling. Standardised on 23 April 1943, it was used only to a limited extent. It was much used by waist gunners for additional protection from the cold air stream. Other than being made of a different material, it had the same features as the AN-H-15.

The B-6 winter and A-9 summer helmets' lack of built-in earphones and outdated design made them unsatisfactory. However, they continued in use for some time, often modified by installing earphone retaining cups as used on the A-11 helmet.

Many of these helmets were phased out by 1943 and only the B-6 winter, A-9 summer, and A-11 intermediate flying helmets were still issued. These in turn were augmented by the AN-H-15 and A-10A summer helmets and the winter AN-H-16 in 1944–45. Other helmets were also used, however. The Royal Canadian Air Force model was more popular in Alaska than issue types; and in England, throughout 1943, the RAF Type C helmet was used extensively by US bomber crews.

The **summer** and **winter training helmets and speaking tube ear piece assembly** both included an integral 'L' shaped metal speaking tube connector assembly over both ears. They were otherwise similar to the A-9 and B-6 helmets in design and materials. These were used during primary flying instruction and attached to a speaking tube connected to the instructor precluding the need for an expensive intercom system in training aircraft.

The **G-1 gunner's auxiliary helmet**, standardised on 26 August 1940, merely provided protection from low-impact blows in the close confinement of bomber tail gun positions; it was not intended for ballistic protection. Its dome-shaped, brown enamelled papier-mâché shell, fitted with a web suspension system, was reinforced with brown leather stripes. Leather snap tabs on the sides and back allowed it to be secured over standard flying helmets. It was eventually superseded by steel helmets.

Electrically heated helmets were tested in the early 1920s, and it was determined that they were unnecessary: since 80% of the body's heat is lost through the head and shoulders, it was found that a properly insulated head-covering provided sufficient protection.

Standard service caps interfered with the use of headsets, so in 1938 the **B-1 summer** and **B-2 winter flying caps** were developed, being standardised on 21 April 1939. Both were a close-fitting ski-type cap made of four front-to-back panels with a pronounced stiff visor. The B-1 was made of light OD gabardine while the B-2 was of seal brown ¼ in. shearling and included a turn-down ear flap, which when not in use was folded to the outside, exposing the fleece. Though popular, B-1 and B-2 were made limited standard on 2 June 1942 and no longer procured after 1944 as they did not integrate well with earphones and oxygen masks. Standard service caps were still worn by some officers, invariably with the crown stiffener removed, along with garrison caps.

Several types of headgear were issued in certain survival kits. An OD **water resistant helmet** with a neck

B-17 waist gunner outfitted in the F-2 electric suit with outer jacket and trousers. Worn with the suit are the F-2 electric gloves, F-2 electric felt shoes and AN-H-16 winter helmet.

securing strap, lined with knitted wool or mouton and similar to a flying helmet, was provided in some arctic and overwater kits. A brimmed **emergency reversible sun hat** was issued in some jungle and tropical overwater kits. It was made of two layers of cotton twill, one side orange-yellow and the other 'camouflaged', either dark OD (jungle kits) or medium blue (overwater kits). It had an adjusting tape threaded through slits in the lower crown. The **parachute emergency kit mosquito head net** was made of light OD mesh with a cotton crown piece.

The **D-1 face mask (cold weather)** was a face-shaped mask secured by an elastic headband, with three cutouts for the eyes and nose/mouth, and made of dark OD felt. Standardised in March 1942, it was intended for crewmen exposed to the air stream, particularly waist gunners, as well as ground crewmen working in outdoor cold weather conditions.

OD wool and white parachute silk **flying scarfs** were also used. The latter prevented exhaled breath from freezing on the scarf when worn over the face. The **N-1 heavy flying scarf** was standardised on 9 November 1944. It was a circular OD wool knit turtleneck, pullover neck protector.

The two-piece F-3 electric suit is modelled here with the Q-1 electric shoe inserts; their electrical connectors can be seen attached to the suit's circuits.

GLOVES AND FOOTWARE

Gloves, often called gauntlets, were crucial for protection not only from extreme cold, but also from injury when working with machinery or weapons and to ensure a firm grip on control sticks and weapons. A survey by VIII Bomber Command in early 1943 showed that hands were the most frequent frostbitten body part constituting 51% of all cases. Some flyers' gloves were of the one- or two-finger mitten design, but most were designated gloves.

The **A-8 winter flying gloves** were standardised on 20 October 1930. These five-finger gloves consisted of a seal brown horsehide shell lined with medium weight camel hair. They were declared obsolete on 31 March 1944. The **A-9 winter flying gloves**, standardised on 22 April 1935, were two-finger (forefinger and thumb) mittens made of seal brown pigskin shell lined with shearling. An improved version, the **A-9A winter flying gloves**, were standardised on 11 April 1944. It was made of goatskin, pony hide, or deerskin lined with shearling. The **A-10 winter flying gloves** were standardised on 20 July 1938. They were made of seal brown goatskin or pony hide, lined with dark brown knit wool, and had exposed knit wristlets. They were replaced by the **A-11 winter flying gloves** on

30 March 1943 due to the A-10's poor fit. The A-11 was made of the same materials, but with removable dark OD knit wool inserts, the wrists of which extended beyond the shells' gauntlets. The 1944 **A-11A winter flying gloves** included take-up elastic in the wrists. These offered protection from 14–50°F. Airmen were encouraged to carry extra inserts to replace sweat-dampened ones. The **A-12 arctic flying gloves** were a one-finger (thumb) mitten with take-up straps on the gauntlets. The shell was made of light OD water-resistant gabardine with brown horsehide palms lined with fleece, or later, wool pile. They were standardised on 30 March 1943 for use with the down-lined B-9/A-8 suit and also kept on-hand for wear over electric gloves in event of power failure.

Dark OD **rayon glove inserts** were developed in 1942 for use by mechanics, but standardised in 1943 for flying personnel to wear with the A-9, -11, -12, and electric gloves; they included knitted wristlets. Besides providing additional insulation, they protected the hands from freezing metal when delicate manipulations precluded the use of heavy gloves. In 1943 wool and rayon inserts began to be made ambidextrous, with the thumb centred on the in-

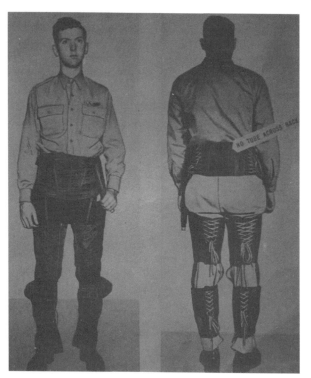

The Clark G-3 fighter pilot's pneumatic suit showing the lacing system. The Berger G-3 anti-G suit, on which the G-3A suit was based, had a longer hose running across the small of the back. This demonstrator holds the short connecting hose in his left hand.

sert's side edge. This permitted the conservation of one insert when the other became unserviceable or was lost.

The **B-2 unlined summer flying gloves** were made of brown lightweight goatskin; standardised on 17 August 1942, limited standard on 23 July 1943. On the same date the **B-3 unlined summer flying gloves** were standardised. Similar to the B-2, they were made of tan deerskin or capeskin with perforated fourchettes and take-up elastic inside the wrists. The **B-3A unlined summer flying gloves**, introduced in 1944, were seal brown and included longer gauntlets with the AAF insignia printed in white on the back of the hands.

The **F-1 anti-exposure gloves** were a component of the R-1 anti-exposure suit. They were one-finger mittens made of two layers of orange-yellow neoprene-coated nylon with an OD knit wool insert.

The **K-1 mosquito resistant very light flying gloves** were intended for wear with the K-1 flying suit and standardised on 4 June 1945. They were made of khaki Byrd with brown leather palms and thumb. The wrists and top of the elbow-length gauntlets had elastic shirring.

Several types of electric heated gloves, with no compatible suits, were developed in the 1920s and '30s, but were not too effective. The only one of these used during the war was the **C-4 electric heated flying gloves** standardised in 1937 and used until 1944. It was a wool knit glove and could be worn alone or inside the A-9 glove. Its wires were rubber covered. They were used by bomber crews prior to the issue of electric suits.

Developed in conjunction with the E-1 and F-1 electric suits were the **C-6 and E-1 electric heated flying gloves**, the C-6 for the 12 volt E-1 suit and the E-1 gloves for the 24 volt F-1 suit. They were standardised on 4 April 1941. These were made with seal brown goatskin or pony hide shells and wool lining containing the heating wires. The back of the hands and wrist gauntlets were also leather-lined. Short electrical connection cords protruded from the wrist openings.

The **F-2 electric heated flying gloves**, for use with the F-2 and F-3/F-3A electric suits, were developed between November 1942 and September 1943. Made of seal brown leather, they had a two-layer, knit wool insert containing the heating wires with either snap stud or bayonet connectors. The F-2 had take-up elastic in the wrists. They offered improved dexterity over earlier electric gloves. Rayon inserts were worn with all electric gloves.

Footwear

Flyers' shoes were designed for maximum protection from the cold, but this led to excessive bulkiness in most types. This resulted in difficulties for pilots when manipulating control pedals, and for ball turret gunners already suffering from a cramped fit. A major concern with flying-shoe design was their suitability for long-distance walking if forced down behind enemy lines, as well as providing airmen with shoes for prolonged imprisonment. Most flyers' footwear were of a boot design, but were designated shoes.

The **A-5 winter flying shoes** were the last of the 'moccasin' style to see service. They were made of seal brown horsehide lined with shearling and had a leather sole. The front was laced and a zipper was installed on the back seam. They were issued on a limited standard basis from 22 May 1935 to 27 March 1944.

The most widely used shoes were the 10 in. high **A-6 winter flying shoes** standardised on 27 March 1937. They were made of seal brown, lacquered ¾ in. shearling with a zippered closure and shearling tongue. The flat, non-skid soles were of black rubber. They could be worn with or without standard service shoes, and could also be worn over electric shoes or special inserts. It was not uncommon for these shoes to be ripped off when parachuting from a high-speed aircraft resulting in frostbite if at high altitudes and injuries upon landing. When retained, it was found that they were entirely unsuited for long-distance

walking. In November 1944, retaining straps were added. This modification was standardised on 7 August 1945 as the **A-6A winter flying shoes** incorporating a buckled, padded, leather retaining strap for securing over the instep and an unpadded one around its top opening to provide a secure fit. The **A-7 winter flying shoes (inserts)** were available for wear with the A-6/A-6A shoes; standardised on 4 December 1937. They were made of natural tan shearling reinforced with brown horsehide seam strips; the sole and heel were made of pressed felt. They were secured by simple tie tapes. Besides the various electrical heated shoes, by 1944 the A-6 was the only flying shoe in wide use.

The **A-8 winter flying shoes** were made of OD canvas lined with shearling. They had a non-skid rubber sole and were lighter and less bulky than the A-6. Standardised on 28 May 1940, they saw only limited use until declared obsolete on 27 March 1944. The **A-9 winter flying shoes** were an intermediate weight type made of slick black rubber, lined with shearling, and with a zippered closure. The flat soles were of non-skid rubber, but the rubber uppers were too hot in temperate zones and too cold in cold climates, so they were seldom used. The A-9 was standardised on 28 April 1941 and made limited standard on 2 June 1942.

Several types of heavy shoes, intended for use in Alaska, were also developed. The **A-10 winter flying shoes** were high top boots made of natural tan shearling reinforced by brown horsehide seam stripes. The soles were of the black rubber 'tire cord' cleat type. An adjust-

P-47 pilot of the 359th Fighter Squadron wearing the G-3A fighter pilot's pneumatic suit over a dark OD A-9 flying suit. He also wears the B-8 goggles and B-4 life vest.

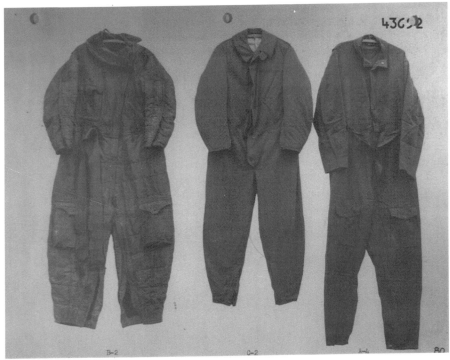

The three suits making up th eold layered, down-filled flotation suit. (left to right) B-2 down-filled suit, C-2 wool-insultated suit, and A-4 summer suit. All are light OD in colour.

An airman demonstrates the R-1 quick-donning anti-exposure suit and the AN-R-2A one-man parachute raft. The suit and raft are orange-yellow, the former has black seam sealing stripes down the front and outer leg seams. 'FRONT' was usually stencilled on the chest. The ¾ lb. CO_2 cylinder and raft accessory packs float alongside. The later C-2 one-man parachute raft had more rounded ends.

able, buckled strap was fitted over the instep and a drawstring ran around the top opening. Though an attempt had been made to design them to accommodate walking, they were too heavy and cumbersome. Standardised on 7 July 1941, they were made substitute standard on 17 August 1942 and issued to ground crews. The **A-11 winter flying shoes (inserts)** were issued with the A-10. They were of the same materials and basic design as the A-7 inserts, but had no soles, being of the slipper type. Standardised on 19 August 1942, the **A-12 winter flying shoes** were developed to provide a design suitable for walking. Similar in style to the heavier A-6, they were made with shearling-lined heavy OD duck uppers with zipper closures and black leather soles. They too were unsuccessful and were declared obsolete on 19 March 1943. The **A-14 arctic flying shoes** were of the mukluk type with 14 in. high, light OD duck uppers and black rubber soles and toe caps. Tabs with four eyelets were fitted to the insteps for lacings. The

The light OD A-9 summer helmet, as worn with the AN-S-31 summer suit, displaying the various retaining tabs and straps for the goggles and radio/intercom headset. Also visible are the adjusting drawstring and chin strap details.

top opening was secured by a drawstring. They were standardised on 26 April 1943. Some difficulty was experienced with the rubber becoming rigid in extreme cold and they were found to be ill suited for flyers. They continued to be used by ground crew personnel, however. With the A-14 was issued the **A-14 shoe insert assembly**: four pairs of progressively larger wool socks, a pair of pressed felt over-slippers, and felt insoles. (The A-14 shoes were an experimental mukluk that was not adopted.)

Standard issue russet brown laced, high top **service shoes**, commonly called GI shoes, were worn inside flying shoes or by themselves by low-altitude flyers. They were of two types: those with smooth leather uppers and a capped toe were for stateside issue (known as 'Blucher' shoes) while those of rough leather and no toe cap were issued overseas. The overseas issue shoes had black reclaimed rubber soles while the stateside issue had this type of sole or a leather sole and rubber heel. It was common for the stateside issue to be worn overseas by flyers. It was common practice for airmen to tie their issue service shoes to their parachute harness. While enabling them to walk if shot down, the practice was felt to be detrimental to morale.

Developed in conjunction with the E-1 and F-1 electric suits were the **C-1** and **D-1 electric heated flying shoes**, actually inserts to be worn inside the A-9 and other flying shoes. Both were standardised on 4 April 1941. The C-1 were for the 12 volt E-1 suit and the D-1 shoes for the 24 volt F-1 suit. These were made of blue or grey felt respectively and lined with moleskin cloth containing the heating wires. They were closed by a four-snap secured flap with electrical connection cords protruding from the tops.

The **F-1 electric heated flying felt shoe inserts** and **F-2 electric heated flying felt shoes**, for use with the F-2 electric suit, were developed between November 1942 and September 1943. They could also be worn with the F-3/F-3A suits. The F-1 inserts, made of dark grey felt,

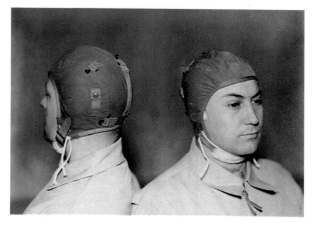

were simple slippers with heating wires sewn to the outer surface and were fastened by snaps: some had felt outsoles. The F-2 shoe was similar to the laced service shoe in appearance and allowed walking. It had a composite material sole and heel with web reinforcements on the heel and instep seams. Its sole heating wires were protected from abrasion by felt insoles and outsoles. The F-2 was used principally by ball turret gunners who did not have room for A-6 shoes and F-1 electric inserts.

The **Q-1 electric heated flying shoe inserts,** for use with the F-2 and F-3/F-3A electric suits, were standardised on 31 October 1944. Made of three layers of dark OD fabric, the heating wires were sewn into the middle layer. The Q-1 was closed by a laced flap and a drawstring around the top. They were designed to be worn inside A-6/A-6A shoes and over standard service shoes. This layering system provided sufficient warmth in the event of power failure as well as permitting the wear of good walking shoes.

Under garments

Worn under all these varied flying clothes were standard service uniforms, determined by the climate on the ground. In Europe, OD wool trousers and wool or cotton flannel shirts were generally worn. In the Pacific, Mediterranean, and other hot/warm theatres cotton khaki shirts and trousers were used, though these were also worn by low altitude flyers during European summers. Cotton khakis also served as flying clothes themselves, with no other outer garments, in hot areas. A study found that airmen desired to wear an appropriate and comfortable uniform under any flying clothes against the possibility of capture and prolonged confinement. While this may sound defeatist it addressed a simple reality, as few flyers managed to evade capture inside enemy territory.

Winter underwear was in the form of long-sleeve undershirts and long underdrawers, of OD, tan or white wool/cotton blend. In the Pacific and other tropical areas, it was common to wear only underwear under summer fly-

This P-51 pilot wears the khaki AN-H-15 summer helmet with HS-38 radio headset and B-7 goggles. The details of the helmet's doeskin-lined chin strap are visible. The parachute harness is that of the S-5 seat type.

ing suits. Summer underwear consisted of OD or white cotton sleeveless undershirts and short underdrawers.

The **C-2 winter flying vest** was actually a 'V' neck, zippered front, long-sleeve sweater made of knitted OD worsted wool with a single patch pocket on the left midriff. It was standardised on 18 June 1934. Of similar design was the **C-3 winter flying vest** standardised on 28 May 1936. It was made of $\frac{3}{8}$ in. shearling, was seal brown, and lacked sleeves and pockets.

Several models of QMC sweaters, issued to all Army branches, were also used, all of OD knit worsted wool or a wool/rayon blend. Two early models were the **sleeveless sweater,** a crew-neck, pullover vest; and the **knit shirt,** a lightweight, long-sleeve sweater with a four-button collar opening. In 1943 a popular long-sleeve, five-button neck closure **highneck sweater** was issued. Many privately purchased sweaters were also used.

The A-11 intermediate helmet. Made of seal brown leather, it was lined only with doeskin, but proved to be sufficiently warm for even high-altitude use. He wears an early version of the A-10 intermediate jacket with shoulder straps.

This B-17 waist gunner wears the AN-H-16 winter helmet with an AN-J-4 intermediate jacket.

Flying clothes insignia

As a rule the wear of insignia on flying clothes was relatively limited. Those few that were worn can be divided into two categories, rank and unit insignia. Seldom were any insignia worn on the winter and intermediate flying jackets, it being difficult to sew through thick shearling. Few insignia were worn on summer flying suits. A white, black or full-colour AAF patch was printed on the left shoulder of later flying suits; usually below this was 'ARMY AIR FORCES' in $\frac{3}{8}$ in. high white letters. Some of these insignia were printed without the wings' orange, the garment's colour showing through, an early form of subdued insignia. Small versions of this insignia were printed or stamped in white on other items such as helmets.

Officers' rank insignia was commonly worn on the A-2 and other lightweight flying jackets. This took two forms, either standard metal insignia directly on the shoulder straps of A-2 jackets (or pinned to russet leather shoulder tabs on other jackets), or simple, flat, cutout metal insignia affixed to russet tabs, specifically for flying jackets and suits; referred to as 'leather insignia'. The tabs were sewn just above the shoulder seam. Though seldom used, non-standard printed, embroidered, or plastic insignia were available. Enlisted men did not normally wear rank markings on flying clothes, with the occasional exception of summer flying suits. They did wear their sleeve chevrons on shirts worn as under garments. Insignia were worn on officers' shirts with the AAF branch of service wings and prop on the left and (initially) the U.S. on the right collar with the rank on the shoulder straps. From August 1942 the rank was removed from the shoulders and replaced the U.S. on the right collar. Officers wished to make certain they could be identified as such if downed over enemy territory.

Unit insignia in the form of squadron, group, or wing patches were sometimes sewn onto the left chest of light-weight flying jackets. These insignia were officially approved for painting on aircraft and their use on flying clothes was semi-official. The often colourful and even humorous insignia were generally circular, though other shapes, especially shields, were common. Walt Disney Studios designed many of these at no cost to the government. They could be printed on leather backings, embroidered and sewn to a leather patch or sewn directly on the jacket. A 5 in. diameter seal brown leather insignia patch was issued for this purpose, but the backing of many odd-shaped and larger insignia followed their outlines. The AAF, numbered air force, or other major organisation's patch was also sewn on the left shoulder of some jackets and summer flying suits, as well as on service shirts.

A leather name plate, a $\frac{5}{8} \times 4$ in. natural tan or light brown strip, was issued on the basis of four per man. The flyer's name, usually initials and last name, was stamped with a punch set issued to units or inked on. The plate was sewn, using pre-punched stitching holes, on the left chest of jackets and summer flying suits. It was sewn above any unit insignia, while aviator wings, if worn, were pinned above the name plate.

FLYERS' EQUIPMENT

The various categories of gear described here all served a single purpose: keeping airmen alive and well in a hostile environment, whether in the air, on the ground, or in the 'drink'. Considerable effort and resources were expended in the attempt. Besides issuing the best possible clothing and equipment, coupled with extensive initial training in their use, the combat replacement centres provided all airmen newly assigned to a theatre with two weeks of area-oriented instruction on flying clothes, parachutes, flak suits, oxygen equipment, first aid, and ditching proced-

Two popular and widely used flying caps. (Top): The light OD gabardine B-1 summer cap. (Bottom): The seal brown shearling B-2 winter cap with the ear flaps down; they could be folded up exposing the fleece lining.

The D-1 face mask, which ▶ *could not be used with an oxygen mask, is worn with the A-11 intermediate helmet and A-2 jacket. This type of rubber earphone retaining cups were used in the later AN-H-15 and -16 helmets and added to B-6 winter helmets.*

ures. Proper care and use of the many and varied flyers' equipments was so critical that non-rated (non-pilots) Personal Equipment Officers (PEO) and enlisted Personal Equipment Technicians (PET) were authorised in flying units in March 1943. PEOs worked closely with unit medical, safety, and oxygen officers to provide instruction in the proper installation, care, and function of protective clothing and emergency equipment.

Besides issue equipment, it was not uncommon for units to develop their own protective and survival gear. (An example of unit-developed gear was a backpack jungle survival kit with an attached one-man raft used by XIII Fighter Command.) While unit-developed items often served a unique need or made up for shortages, difficulties were occasionally encountered due to insufficient testing or unsuitable materials.

Equipment will sometimes be found with a conspicuous one to three digit number stencilled on it. These were usually items that were stored outside an individual airman's locker, e.g. kit bag, oxygen mask, life vest, electric heated suit. In some units certain equipment items, e.g. flak jackets or electric suits, were pooled for use by several individuals if sufficient quantities were not available. These too were marked with numbers.

The equipment described here was used by individual airmen, we do not address equipments intended for groups of personnel such as multiplace life rafts and crew survival kits.

Parachutes

AAF (and later US Air Force) parachutes were designated by type letters identifying the position in which they were worn. A—chest, B—back, S—seat, T—training or troop.

The latter, used by paratroopers, were composed of a main backpack and a chest-mounted reserve. Though this system was retained, some parachutes were redesignated, with slight modification, under the 1942 Army-Navy standardisation programme. Since the differences between the original AAF models and the AN versions were so slight, they will be discussed here together. There were also many minor manufacturing modifications to parachute pack assemblies, harnesses, and canopies, far too numerous to discuss here. There were even differences between the AN standardised parachutes with minor construction refinements preferred by both services. Army versions' AN drawing numbers were followed by '-1' while the Navy's had '-2'.

The development and testing of parachutes had been conducted by the Engineering (later Material) Division's Parachute Branch at McCook Field, Ohio, since 1919. The use of parachutes by aviators was made compulsory in 1921. In 1927 the Material Division was moved to the nearby, new Wright Field and parachute development was continued under the Experimental Engineering Section.

The use of the different types of parachutes depended on the flyers' crew position or type of aircraft. Most large aircraft, bombers and transports, permitted the use of the

B-17 waist gunner wearing the A-9 winter gloves and an AN-H-16 winter helmet.

Two AN6020-1 walk-around bottles can be seen under the gun's feed chute.

acted as a 'seat' for the ride down, and permitted the attachment of survival gear. Harnesses were originally made of natural (white) linen Type VII webbing with a breaking strength of 2,800 lbs. and a life of two years. White cotton webbing with a similar breaking strength, and much longer service life, replaced linen before the war. This in turn was replaced by white cotton webbing with nylon filling (reinforced), first procured in early 1942, principally to reduce swelling in harness hardware; this had a breaking strength of 2,900 lbs. Late in the war dark OD and brown webbing were used. All of these webbing types were 1¾ in. wide; cotton and cotton/nylon webbing had a black identifying yarn woven into the centre.

Harnesses were fitted with a back pad cushion, the design depending on the type of parachute. Pads were OD canvas covered and filled with bound hair or foam rubber. These could be replaced with emergency parachute back pad containers containing survival gear (see Emergency Kits).

Until 1944 emergency parachute harnesses were of the adjustable three-point connection type; a single chest strap and two leg straps that connected to the main harness assembly. The British-developed single-point, quick release box (QRB), called the 'Irvin type box' after the manufacturer, was first tested by the US in the mid-1930s; a fatal test jump in 1941 precluded its planned adoption. It was composed of an assembly allowing the chest and leg straps to be snapped into a single fitting on the wearer's chest. By rotating, to unlock, and then slapping the circular release plate, all straps were released, permitting rapid removal of the harness. Development by the British was influenced by their extensive overwater flight requirements, as it allowed rapid removal in the water; this was not then considered a major concern by the US. In early 1943 VIII Bomber Command was using 2,500 British parachutes with the QRB, and requested the device be incorporated into US models; this was again rejected because of perceived safety, manufacturing, and maintenance difficulties. However, in late 1943 a safety fork, copied from the German version of the QRB, was adopted and orders were placed in March 1944 for redesigned harnesses incorporating the release, though there were still some flaws in the design.

Hardware fittings were made of aircraft quality drop forged alloy steel. Spring-loaded snap hooks were coupled to 'V' rings for the chest and leg strap connections, both with a 2,500 lb. tensile strength. The larger snap hooks on early chest packs were coupled to 'D' rings attached to the harness, both with a 5,000 lb. tensile strength. From 1943 QAC type harnesses (A3 parachute and later types) had the 'D' rings on the pack's back and snap hooks on the risers. Some earlier model parachutes still in use had bayonet type harness fasteners—a male-female, twist and lock fitting

flexible back type parachutes, which conform to the wearer's back contour. Though intended to be worn at all times while airborne, they were sometimes stowed near the crewman's station or exit during non-combat sorties for comfort or ease of movement. Bomber crewmen operating in confined positions or requiring additional mobility used quick attachable chest (QAC) parachutes: rather than removing the entire parachute assembly, QAC parachutes permitted airmen to wear the harness and remove only the parachute pack, which could be quickly snapped on if needed. They were stowed near their emergency exit together with a one-man life-raft. Ball turret, tail, and waist gunners used these extensively. Fighter pilots preferred seat parachutes (which allowed the head to be turned more freely), though in the Pacific, most used back types since seat parachutes were uncomfortable on long flights.

Parachute pack assemblies were made of 12.29 oz. per sq.yd. cotton duck, either light OD or the later dark OD. The pack contained and protected the canopy; it had internal loops in which the suspension lines were stowed and elastic pack opening cords, and included the ripcord fittings. Pack opening cords were made of ³⁄₁₆ in. diameter elastic, white or dark OD with black threads.

The harness served to fasten the pack to the airman,

with a 2,000 lb. tensile strength. Rectangular adjusting strap adapters, fitted at the harness shoulders, had a 1,000 lbs. tensile strength. Connector links, linking the suspension lines to the harnesses' riser straps, had either a 1,500 or 3,000 lb. tensile strength. Parachute suspension lines were permanently fastened to the harness risers (no canopy releases were used as on today's parachutes, to allow the jumper to jettison the canopy in water or when being dragged by high ground winds). Back and seat parachute ripcord housings were made of flexible, coiled stainless steel tubing.

Prior to the war all parachute canopies and suspension lines were fabricated of japanese silk, 1.75 oz. per sq.yd. In anticipation that a conflict with Japan would cut off supplies from the Far East, the Air Corps began experiments with substitute materials as early as 1927. These initially included cotton (too bulky, lacked sufficient tensile strength, slow opening) and domestic silk. Domestic output was limited and more costly; but it was standardised for emergency war production in 1930. Silk canopies had a service life of five years, unless used in the tropics which reduced it to two years. Rayon was tested in 1929–30 and was also standardised for emergency war production if sufficient silk was not available, but lacked silk's strength and elasticity. Nylon was tested in 1939 and compared favourably with silk, being stronger, but slightly bulkier. The first nylon canopies and suspension lines were procured in late 1941. Improvements in the synthetic were made and additional nylon canopies were ordered in early 1942; the last silk canopies were made in the spring of 1943. Nylon 16 oz. per sq.yd. twill also has the benefit of not deteriorating as rapidly with age (service life was seven years), though it is damaged by prolonged exposure to sunlight. Nylon also absorbs little water, dries quickly, and is not damaged by salt water. The extensive demand on America's fledgling nylon industry did have the drawback of requiring the same amount of nylon as 500 pairs of ladies' stockings for one parachute. The hundreds of thousands of parachutes required explains the severe wartime shortage of that commodity, so often commented on in motion pictures.

The basic emergency parachute canopy was the 24 ft. diameter flat circular design; its 452 sq.ft. of nylon was constructed of 24 gores (pie-slice shaped segments) of four panels each. Twelve continuous, nylon 375 lb. test suspension lines (silk lines were 450 lb.) were sewn into the gore seams providing 24 lines attached to the harness riser straps. Limited use was made of an identically designed 28

ft. diameter, 616 sq.ft. 28 gore and line canopy with some seat type parachutes (for use by men over 180 lbs.). Canopies were solid white, and although OD and camouflage canopies were considered, they were not adopted. Attached to the apex of all emergency canopies was a white 28, 30, or 36 in. spring-loaded 'spider' pilot parachute to aid extraction from the pack. Standard 24 ft. canopies were identified by drawing number 42G2001-series while the 28 ft. were the 42J2019-series. Parachute assemblies weighed 18–22 lb., the QAC and seat types being slightly lighter than back types.

Quick attachable chest type parachutes were designated either as Group 1 red or Group 2 yellow, the two groups' packs and harnesses not being interchangeable. The harnesses and chest packs' ripcord protector flaps were marked with the appropriate colour to ensure a correct match. The **A-2 parachute** (from 1942, AN6513–1 and -1A) was a QAC model standardised on 6 November 1936 and the only type designated in Group 1 red. The two-pin, short cable ripcord handle was on the wearer's right end of the rectangular pack. When the canopy inflated, the risers suspended the jumper by the chest causing a head-back attitude and resultant landing difficulties. Its harness had 'D' rings mounted on the vertical chest straps to which the pack was attached by snap hooks. Some British chest parachutes incorporating the single-point QRB were used by the Eighth AF and proved to be very

A C-54 pilot wearing A-12 arctic gloves (actually one-finger mittens) made of light OD gabardine with brown leather palms and lined with fleece. He also wears an A-11 intermediate helmet and B-15 intermediate jacket.

A navigator, operating an AN5738-1 astro compass, wears the F-2 electric heated gloves with an AN- H-16 winter helmet, and the F-2 electric suit's outer jacket.

popular. With an increased need for QAC parachutes in 1942, and the desire for the jumper to be suspended by the shoulders as with other parachutes, the **A-3 parachute** was developed. This, and all subsequent types (Group 2 yellow), had the 'D' rings on the pack's back and snap hooks on the risers, which were clipped to the shoulder straps. When opened, the container was pulled up above the jumper with the risers, though jumpers were sometimes smacked in the face by the pack. It offered shoulder suspension, but still featured a three-point connection rather than the desired single-point QRB, and was little used. The **A-4 parachute**, standardised on 14 December 1944, incorporated the QRB. A design flaw prevented its release (desirable when landing in water) while bearing the jumper's weight, was uncomfortable, and the riser snap hooks sometimes caused head injuries during opening. The **A-5 parachute**, incorporating the desired QRB and harness improvements, was standardised on 5 January 1945.

The **B-4 and B-5 parachutes** were standardised on 31 August 1939 and 15 March 1940 respectively. Both were improvements over earlier models, but were outclassed by the B-7. Both were made limited standard in 1940, saw

little use in the war and were declared obsolete in 1942 and 1944 respectively. The **B-7 parachute** (from 1942, AN6512–1 and –1A) was a back type standardised on 1 October 1940. It used a three-pin ripcord (all back types had the handles on the left side of the harness) and a buckled waist band integral to the pack and in addition to the three-point connection (deleted on the later AN6512–1); many had old bayonet-type harness fasteners. Its harness and pack were uncomfortable and it was replaced by the **B-8 parachute** standardised in late 1942. B-7s continued to be used though. The B-8 had a more comfortable harness and soft pack, moulding to the contour of the wearer's back, deleted the waist band, and used a four-pin ripcord. Some early harnesses used bayonet fasteners, but most had snap hooks. A small number were modified with a larger container to accommodate the 28 ft. canopy. The **B-9 parachute** was standardised on 1 January 1944, using the B-8s soft pack, but with a single-point QRB harness connection, which caused the same release difficulties as the A-4; improper fitting could also cause groin injuries, and the riser adapters sometimes inflicted head injuries during opening. The **B-10 parachute** was standardised on 5 January 1945 using the B-8 container, an improved QRB and harness, and was the first parachute to feature a ripstop nylon canopy.

While all QAC and back type parachutes in use at the beginning of the war were recent designs, the then current seat models were of much earlier origin. All seat types had a 2 in. thick seat cushion made of OD duck-covered sponge rubber. In 1943 these were replaced by bound hair-filled cushions due to the rubber shortage that year. Even though the rubber cushions had replaced a pneumatic model in early 1939, this model was sought by pilots in the Pacific flying long-range missions, due to its comfort. Special seat pads for survival gear were also used (see Emergency Kits). All seat types were fitted with a two-pin, long cable ripcord with the handle on the left side of the harness.

The **S-1 parachute** (from 1942, AN6510–1), standardised on 11 May 1928, used a 24 ft. canopy. The **S-2 parachute** (AN6511–1) was standardised on 19 June 1929 and identical to the S-1 except for a 28 ft. canopy. Both were used through the war. (The S-3 of 1932 used a 23 ft. triangular canopy and was dropped from use prior to the war due to production, packing, and maintenance problems. The S-4 suffered problems and was withdrawn from service in 1935.) The **S-5 parachute** was standardised 29 December 1943. It used the QRB, but like the A-4 and B-9, was uncomfortable and still difficult to open under load. (The S-6 parachute, with an improved QRB and new harness, did not come out until 1946.)

Parachutes and other gear were carried to and from the aircraft in the pre-war **A-1**, **-2**, and **3 flyer's kit** *or* **para-**

chute travelling bags and the 1943 **AN6505–1 aviator's kit bag**. The latter replaced the A-3 and is still in use today. They were issued on the basis of one per air crewman. All models were similar in design and made of OD duck measuring 13 in. wide, 18¾ in. deep, and 22½ in. long. All were fitted with two web carrying handles and a two-way zipper; a small padlock was issued with the bags.

Goggles and sun glasses

Two types of flying goggles were in common use at the outbreak of war. The **B-6 flying goggle assembly** was standardised on 1 August 1928. It was an adopted commercial design with a single curved lens and cushioned frame. It was made limited standard on 3 May 1933 and used principally in the States until declared obsolete on 13 March 1944. The **B-7 flying goggle assembly**, standardised on 3 May 1933, was composed of a grey chamois, sponge-rubber-lined assembly with two metal, hinged lens retaining frames and an adjustable elastic headband. It was available with amber, clear, or anti-glare green lens. Many minor variants of this mask were made to include the AN6530 adopted in early 1943. Made limited standard on 13 October 1943, the B-7 was available for issue only in the States due to its restrictive field of vision, tendency to fog, and poor integration with oxygen masks.

The 1942 **flying type all purpose goggle assembly** had a one-piece lens held in a grey moulded, synthetic rubber frame fitted with an elastic headband. Made by Polaroid Corp., it was issued with either a non-polarizing plastic amber lens (for hazy or foggy weather) or red lens (primarily for use by gunners, the better to observe tracers in daylight, and for pre-mission dark adaptation).

The **B-8 goggle kit** was standardised on 13 October 1943 to better integrate with oxygen masks. It had an improved rubber frame and was issued with interchangeable lenses: three clear, four light green, and two amber, which could be worn singly or in combination. An electric heated lens was also developed and issued, with a cord and adaptors for plugging into the different types of electric heated suits.

The **E-1 dark adaptation goggle** was standardised on 11 March 1943 and fitted with two-piece red lenses in a lightweight, folding light brown leather frame. The **H-1 eye protective goggle**, standardised on 4 August 1944, was issued in the C-1 emergency vest and other survival kits, as were different QMC issue models. They were similar in design to the E-1, but had green lenses in a leather or fabric frame. The E-1 and H-1 were based on the QMC M1943 goggle issued to ground troops.

The American Optical Co. **D-1 flying goggle assembly**, standardised on 13 August 1935, was actually a pair of sun glasses with a rigid frame and plastic insulated arms. It was superseded by the more comfortable **flying sun glasses (comfort cable)** in November 1941. Both had light green anti-glare lenses and metal frames. The American Optical Co., **Polaroid flying goggle assembly**, again, actually sun glasses, was used to defeat extreme glare in snow-covered and desert regions. Its dark amber lenses were held in either an amber or clear plastic frame. The **Type 2 flying sun glasses**, with rose smoke lenses, was adopted in late 1944, but was not issued until after all existing stocks of sun glasses with green lens were expended. The Type 2 was similar in design to the comfort cable type. It was found that the dark rose lenses provided better protection from brilliant sky illumination than light green. Its replaceable lenses were interchangeable with those of the F-1 sun goggles used by AAF ground personnel.

In late 1943 there was a shortage of medically qualified men to fill the very heavy bomber programme. Technically skilled men, not meeting vision requirements, were fitted with corrective lenses, both ordinary and sun glasses, and employed in B-29 crews.

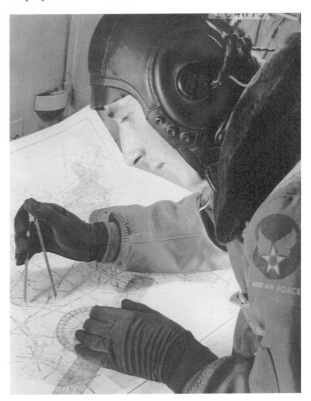

Details of the dark OD rayon glove inserts can be seen here along with an A-11 intermediate helmet with oxygen mask adapter snaps fitted. The glove inserts were worn inside most flying gloves. He is wearing the A-15 intermediate jacket displaying the full-colour printed AAF insignia.

Oxygen masks

Face masks for dispensing breathing oxygen were a critical item of aviators' equipment. Oxygen had to be used above 10,000 ft. or an airman would suffer from anoxia (oxygen starvation) impairing efficiency and judgement, and at 25,000 ft. bombing altitudes, causing death. An airman with defective or improperly used oxygen equipment did not realize that he was suffering from anoxia and could easily succumb to the hazard, especially those in remote gunner's positions. Aircrews executing night missions would go on oxygen upon take-off, as it improved night vision.

A great deal of research effort was expended by the Aero Medical Lab to develop reliable and effective masks. Fatalities and injuries caused by defective, damaged, frozen, and misused oxygen masks were a major concern, especially in high-altitude bombers over Europe. Few problems were encountered with oxygen equipment in other theatres due to generally milder conditions. Face masks and their hoses were made of synthetic rubber such as government rubber-styrene (GR-S) and were black (A-7, -8), light grey (A-9, -10), or medium green (A-13, -14, -15). The hose connected to a regulator fitted to the aircraft oxygen system or 'walk-around' assembly.

In November 1942 a second mask was issued to all bomber crewmen to provide a spare in the event of a frozen mask, a common danger. With each mask was issued an OD duck **oxygen mask container assembly**. This flat $6\frac{1}{8} \times 8\frac{1}{8}$ in. pouch was closed by a lift-the-dot snap secured, 'V'-shaped flap.

The **A-7 nasal oxygen mask** had a bulbous nosepiece with a 'Y'-shaped oxygen tube from which a rubber rebreather bag hung, and was secured by a single head strap. Unlike later masks, the A-7's facepiece did not cover the mouth permitting one to speak on a T-17 hand microphone. It was standardised on 15 July 1939 to replace the old full-face leather oxygen masks. It was replaced by the **A-7A** mask on 5 June 1943 and, later, the **A-7B** on 9 June 1945; these saw only very limited use.

The **A-8 oxygen mask**, as the A-7, was of the continuous flow type providing a steady oxygen flow regardless of the wearer's needs. The oxygen flow had to be adjusted by the crewman with the pilot calling out the altitude. It was standardised on 1 May 1940. Highly prone to freezing, they were deemed unsafe early in the European bombing campaign and replacements were rushed to units. A 55 in. long, $\frac{13}{32}$ in. diameter rubber hose connected the mask to the oxygen supply. The facepiece was held in place by a leather strap assembly secured around the nape of the neck; no modification was required to the helmet. It was issued in only one size. In cold weather or at extremely high altitudes, a dark OD wool-lined cotton shield assembly was required to protect the bag from freezing. Due to the A-8's problems, modifications were undertaken resulting in the **A-8A** standardised on 13 February 1941, the **A-8B** of 3 November 1941, and the **A-8C** of 26 January 1945. An attempt was made in 1945 to convert A-8B masks to a demand type, but was only marginally successful. These later A-8s were used only in cargo aircraft.

The **A-9 oxygen mask**, standardised on 9 December 1941, was improved over the A-8 masks in that it was of the straight demand regulator type—i.e. it would supply a flow of oxygen as required by the wearer due to increased activity; a diaphragm-operated flow valve in the oxygen system's regulator supplied the flyer with the proper mixture of air and oxygen according to altitude every time he inhaled, and shut off when he exhaled. The A-9 was made in two sizes, short and long. Its poor fit resulted in it seeing only limited use through early 1942.

One of the most widely used masks was the **A-10 oxygen mask** standardised on 20 April 1942. It was similar to the A-9 in operating principle and appearance, but slightly improved. Procurement of the A-10 was rushed in 1943 as bomber crews in England were still using the deficient A-8. Several improvements were incorporated in the A-10 during the war. An early modification was the **A-10 (converted)** of mid-1942. The **A-10R** (Revised) was adopted in late 1942 to be followed by the **A-10A** in October 1943. The A-10 and A-10A came in three sizes, small, standard, and large. The **A-10R** was issued in four sizes with the addition of extra small. Limited use was made of the **AN-M-3 (AN6001–1) oxygen mask** standardised on 1 July 1943 to replace the A-10, to which it was similar. This joint

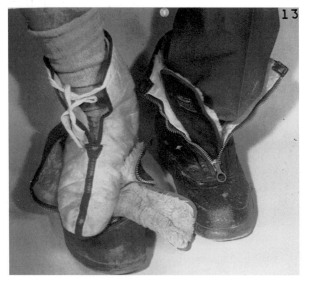

13

The A-6 winter shoes' companion A-7 winter shoes (inserts) are displayed here. The A-6's ¾ in. thick fleece lining is visible.

1: P-39 pilot, 77th Pursuit Sqn.; USA, 1941
2,3: B-18 crewmen, 40th Bomb. Sqn.; USA, 1941
4: GHQAF patch

A

1, 2: B-17E crewmen, 340th Bomb. Sqn.; ETO, 1942
3a: VIII Bomber Command patch
3b: 8th AF patch
4: B-26 crewman, 77th Bomb. Sqn.; Aleutians, 1942
5: 11th AF patch

3b

3a

5

B

1: C-47 pilot, 42nd Transport Sqn.; Alaska, 1942
2: Ferry pilot, North Atlantic Wing, 1943
3a: ACFC, AFFC patch
3b: AFATC patch
4: Bomber crewman, 3rd Search Attack Sqn.; USA, 1943

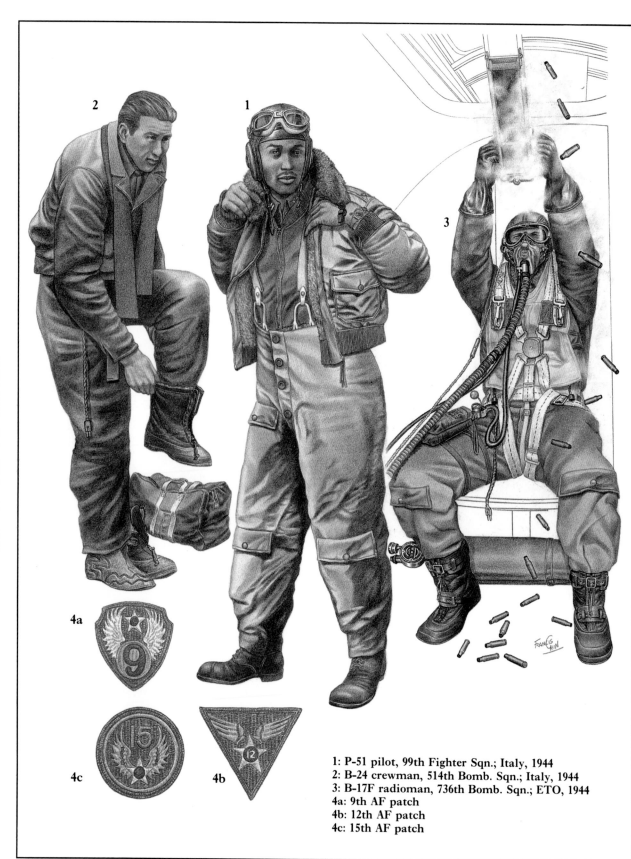

1: P-51 pilot, 99th Fighter Sqn.; Italy, 1944
2: B-24 crewman, 514th Bomb. Sqn.; Italy, 1944
3: B-17F radioman, 736th Bomb. Sqn.; ETO, 1944
4a: 9th AF patch
4b: 12th AF patch
4c: 15th AF patch

D

1: Pilot, 14th Photo. Recce Sqn.; ETO, 1944
2: Bomber crewman, 748th Bomb. Sqn.; ETO, 1944
3: Bomber navigator, 335th Bomb. Sqn.; ETO, 1945
4a,4b: Variants, AAF patch

E

Bailing out:
1: B-17E tail gunner, 1943
2: Bomber crewman, 1944
3: P-51 pilot, 1945

F

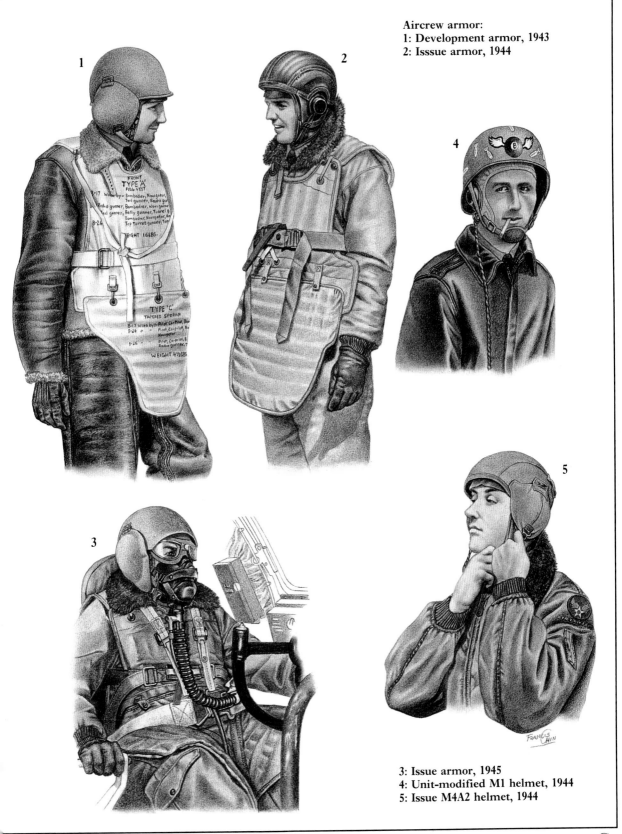

Aircrew armor:
1: Development armor, 1943
2: Isssue armor, 1944

3: Issue armor, 1945
4: Unit-modified M1 helmet, 1944
5: Issue M4A2 helmet, 1944

G

1: P-40 pilot, 44th Fighter Sqn.; Pacific, 1943
2: P-38 pilot, 402nd Fighter Sqn.; ETO, 1944
3: B-25 crewman, 8th Bomb. Sqn.; Pacific, 1944

4a: 5th AF patch. 4b: 10th AF
4c: 13th AF   4d: 14th AF
4e: 20th AF

H

2a

2b

2c

1

1: P-51 pilot, 1st Fighter Sqn.
   (Commando): Asia, 1944
2a: Jacket art, 90th Bomb. Group
2b: Jacket art, 390th Bomb. Group
2c: Jacket art, P-61 night fighter

I

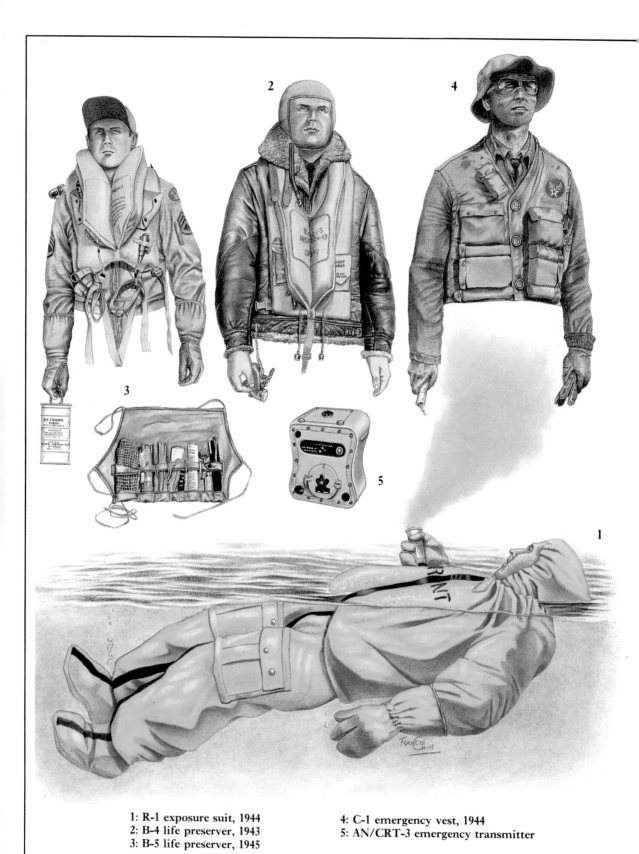

1: R-1 exposure suit, 1944
2: B-4 life preserver, 1943
3: B-5 life preserver, 1945

4: C-1 emergency vest, 1944
5: AN/CRT-3 emergency transmitter

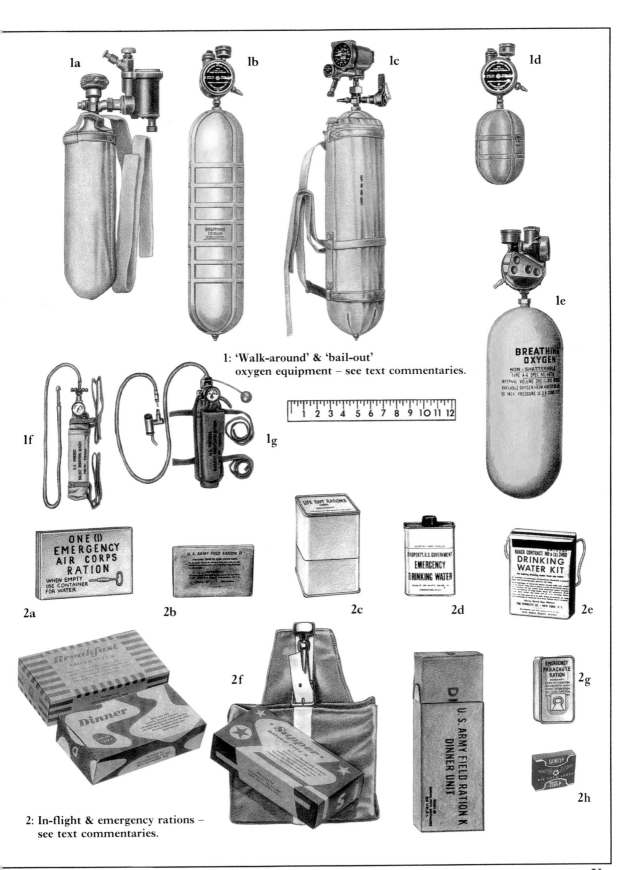

1a 1b 1c 1d

1: 'Walk-around' & 'bail-out'
oxygen equipment – see text commentaries.

1e

1f 1g

BREATHING
OXYGEN
NON - SHATTERABLE
TYPE A-6 SPEC. NO. 40734
INTERNAL VOLUME 280 CUBIC INCH
AVAILABLE OXYGEN FROM 400 TO 30.00
90 INCH PRESSURE IS 2.9 CUBIC FEET

ONE (1)
EMERGENCY
AIR CORPS
RATION
WHEN EMPTY
USE CONTAINER
FOR WATER

U. S. ARMY FIELD RATION D

LIFE RAFT RATIONS

PROPERTY.U.S. GOVERNMENT
EMERGENCY
DRINKING WATER

BUAER CONTRACT NO 8 (s) 2460
DRINKING
WATER KIT

2a 2b 2c 2d 2e

Breakfast
Dinner

2f

U. S. ARMY FIELD RATION K
DINNER UNIT

EMERGENCY
PARACHUTE
RATION
2g

CANDY
2h

2: In-flight & emergency rations –
see text commentaries.

B-17E bail-out, 1943
1, 2: Waist gunners
3: Radio operator –
  see text commentaries.

L

Army-Navy mask was reclassified as limited standard on 15 October 1943 when the A-10A was standardised. (The A-11 and A-12 masks of 1943 were experimental plastic oxygen helmets.)

The **A-14 oxygen mask**, standardised on 1 July 1943, offered greater improvements over the A-10R including more reliable operation and simpler construction, and was less prone to freezing, which still plagued the earlier types. It was first issued to the Eighth AF in early 1943, prior to its standardisation, to replace all earlier types. However, it was found that A-14s still froze. This problem was corrected by a simple modification and most had been fixed by late 1944. The further improved **A-14A** was standardised on 27 January 1945. They were issued in three sizes, small, medium, and large.

The **A-13 oxygen mask** was procured on a limited basis in January 1944 as the standard pressure-demand breathing mask to permit ascent above 40,000 ft. It was designed to hold positive pressure without leakage until the wearer exhaled. The improved **A-13A** was standardised on 28 August 1944. These were used by high-altitude photo-reconnaissance pilots and B-29 bomber crews in lieu of the A-14. However, though designed to fit a wider range of face sizes, they proved to be too tight-fitting on many men, obstructed vision by protruding too far from the face, and made it difficult to speak due to the internal pressure. The **A-15A oxygen mask** (the A-15 was tested, but did not see service) was an improved version of the A-13A and differed only in suspension, a better fit, internal refinements, and could also be used as a demand mask. It saw service use from May 1945, but was not standardised.

With the exception of the A-7 and -8, these masks required the installation of special snaps to flying helmets for attachment. All demand masks used corrugated oxygen supply tubes fitted with standard quick-disconnect connectors. The A-7 and -8 masks had no integral microphones. The A-9 used either MC-253 or -254 microphones. All other models used either the T-42 (carbon), T-44 (magnetic), or ANB-M-C1 (carbon). With the A-8, and in aircraft not needing oxygen masks, a T-30 throat microphone was used.

Oxygen cylinder assemblies

Aviator's breathing oxygen cylinders of many capacities were fitted inside aircraft. These were orange-yellow painted, stainless steel cylinders with 'BREATHING OXYGEN' stencilled in black along with capacity and pressurisation instructions. Cylinders were of two types, high- and low-pressure. High-pressure cylinders posed a hazard when struck by bullets or flak fragments resulting in an explosion throwing out steel shards, and were also a fire hazard. The AAF ceased the development of such cylinders in 1942 and began to use low-pressure types[1]. Early low-pressure cylinders were made of stainless steel reinforced by external strapping which sufficiently supported the cylinder to withstand impact by a .50-cal. bullet. In 1943 low-alloy steel cylinders were developed that eliminated the need for the strapping, were even less affected by gunfire, and marked 'NON-SHATTERABLE' since they looked like the old high-pressure types.

Portable or 'walk-around' cylinders permitted an airman to move about at high altitudes in parts of the aircraft remote from fixed oxygen facilities and beyond reach of extension hoses. The airman disconnected his mask hose from the demand regulator at his crew station and inserted it into the walk-around cylinder's connector. The low-pressure models could be recharged by inserting the regulator spud into a filling valve from the airman's walk-around unit recharger assembly located at his station. (High-pressure and bail-out bottles had to be refilled by ground maintenance personnel.) They were also used to provide emergency oxygen to wounded crew and to revive those in an anoxic state; continuous flow equipment was

[1] The US Navy, RAF, and *Luftwaffe* continued to use high-pressure equipment.

B-17 tail gunner emerging from his escape hatch wearing the dark grey F-2 electric heated flying felt shoes, with tan composite material soles and heels. He is wearing the F-2 electric suit's outer jacket and trousers.

'Leather insignia', actually flat metal cut-outs mounted on russet leather tabs, for wear on the shoulders of flying jackets. All are silver-coloured except major and 2nd lieutenant which are gold-coloured. Their stock numbers are shown beneath. (Top, l. to r.): Brigadier General, Colonel (left shoulder), Colonel (right shoulder), Lieutenant Colonel. Bottom: Major, Captain, 1st Lieutenant, 2nd Lieutenant.

considered better for this purpose. They were also used in event of failure of the main oxygen system and even for escaping from an aircraft underwater. Walk-around cylinders were painted orange-yellow and had black markings, though the A-4 cylinder, used with the AN6020–1 unit, was green.

The 1939 **high-pressure continuous flow walk around assembly** was comprised of a 96 cu. in. (internal volume) A-2 high-pressure cylinder coupled with an A-8A regulator and a walk-around sling, a light OD canvas cylinder-shaped bag and carrying strap. With the introduction of demand type masks, it was found that this assembly provided only two to five minutes of oxygen at 25,000 ft. rather than the required 30–45 minutes.

To provide sufficient oxygen a new assembly, the **low-pressure continuous flow walk around assembly**, was issued in 1942. It was made up of a much larger 500 cu. in., banded D-2 low-pressure cylinder and an A-9A regulator along with a walk-around sling, and was generally slung across the back. It was good for 30 minutes at 25,000 feet.

An improved version of this type of assembly was issued in early 1944. The **low-pressure demand walk around assembly**, or cylinder and sling assembly-portable oxygen, consisted of a D-2 low-pressure cylinder with an A-13 regulator. It used the same sling and had the same duration as the continuous flow version.

The early 1942 **AN6020–1 low-pressure demand walk around unit**, or cylinder and regulator assembly-oxygen portable, was composed of a 104 cu. in. A-4 low-pressure 'football' cylinder and A-13 demand regulator. This small unit had a clip allowing it to be attached to the jacket. It lasted only six to twelve minutes due to its small size and lack of a diluter regulator; it was replaced in 1944 by the following unit.

Maj.Gen. Henry H. 'Hap' Arnold, later commanding general of the USAAF, demonstrates the wear of unit insignia (printed on a leather patch) and leather name plate on the A-2 jacket.

The **regulator and cylinder assembly-diluter demand oxygen** was made up of an A-15 diluter demand regulator and a non-shatterable, 280 cu. in. A-6 low-pressure cylinder. It held a 30-minute oxygen supply, in spite of its small size, because of the diluter feature. It had a clip to attach it to the flying jacket.

Emergency, or bail-out, bottles enabled an airman to take an oxygen supply with him in event of bail-out between 25,000 and 40,000 ft. They were carried in a dedicated pocket on the left side of the flying trousers and also provided with a duck carrying sling with tie-tapes to strap it to the thigh or parachute harness leg strap. A tube storage pocket was part of the sling assembly. Both types included 20 cu. in. high-pressure bottles holding eight to ten minutes of oxygen and were painted green with black markings. They had a pressure gauge and a 2 ft. rubber tube; there was no regulator.

The **H-1 emergency oxygen cylinder assembly**, standardised on 2 October 1941, had a pipe stem on the tube's end. This was thrust under the airman's oxygen

mask into the corner of his mouth and between his back teeth. The oxygen flow was started by a hand-operated valve prior to bail-out. The mask was not to be removed until the airman had descended to a lower altitude. The time and effort to properly insert the pipe stem and manually turn on the flow during a frantic emergency bail-out caused difficulties for many.

The **H-2 emergency oxygen cylinder assembly** was similar to the H-1 but had a non-shatterable cylinder, metering device, and a pull-cable oxygen release fitted with a green-painted wood ball-handle ('green apple'). It was standardised on 20 April 1943. An adaptor was issued with the assembly that fitted between the face-piece and hose of demand masks. The H-2's hose was snapped into the adapter prior to take-off and the cable release simply yanked to begin the oxygen flow upon bail-out.

Body armour

By early October 1942 sufficient data had been collected on projectile wounds among US bomber crews in England to establish that about 70% of the casualties were caused by low velocity projectiles, namely flak fragments and secondary missiles (aircraft structural components, plexiglass, etc.). Brig. Gen. Malcolm C. Grow, Eighth AF Surgeon (later Surgeon General of the US Air Force), became the prime motivating force behind the development of flyers' body armour[1], and many other initiatives aimed at improving the protection and effectiveness of airmen.

Development of flyers' body armour, or 'flak suits', was

[1] For further information on flyers' body armour, see MAA 157, *Flak Jacket.*

begun by the Eighth AF in October 1942. By March 1943 test sets of armour were provided to 12 B-17 crews and the results were encouraging. The Eighth AF commanding general indorsed Gen. Grow's recommendation that the armour be adopted. The Wilkinson Sword Co. produced 600 sets in Britain while much larger contracts were let in the States. The British-produced armour was not available until August 1943, and US production was rushed to meet the demand for enough armour to equip 60% of the Eighth and Ninth AF bomber crews. The body armour was maintained in unit pools and issued to crews prior to a mission and turned in upon return. This 60% figure was the ratio of bombers usually available for operational missions at any one time and enabled all crewmen to be outfitted with a flak suit. By January 1944 the suits had been issued to the Eighth and Ninth AFs in Europe, the Twelfth and Fifteenth in the Mediterranean area, and the Fifth and Thirteenth in the Pacific (where its wear was less common due to a limited flak threat), followed later by the Twentieth AF with its B-29s. The wearing of flak suits and steel helmets reduced fragmentation and bullet fatalities by about 50% and injuries by 70%. Well over half the individuals struck by missiles while wearing armour survived unscathed.

There was initially much resistance to wearing the suits due to their weight and restriction to movement. Some crewmen stood or sat on the vests rather than wearing them, under the mistaken impression that most fragments penetrated the aircraft from below; side penetration was actually much more common. Intensive training, distribution of 'satisfied customer' statements by men wearing vests when hit, and surgeons' reports, accompanied by explicit photos, along with practical experience, eventually convinced most crews that the fatigue and discomfort caused by the suits was worth it.

The suits were made of overlapping 2 in. sq., 0.045 in. (20 gauge) thick Hadfield manganese steel plates sewn into pockets lined with a white cotton fleece-like fabric and covered with light or dark OD duck (early British-made suits were white). Early suits had a list of what crew positions wore which suit components, by type of aircraft, printed on the front. The vests were large enough to be worn over back type parachutes, and were fitted with a quick release system attached by web tapes to shoulder releases. Pulling a red web strap at the midriff caused the entire suit assembly to drop away, allowing the unencumbered flyer to exit the aircraft.

Four body armour components were initially made available. Which components were worn by a specific individual depended on his crew position. British-made components were designated 'type' followed by 'A to D'. The initial US-made components were designated 'T' (Test) followed by '1 to 4'. On 5 October 1943 the test components were standardised and redesignated with an 'M' (Model) followed by the same number. The weights given are for the standardised models, earlier versions' weight varied slightly either way.

The **M1 flyer's armour vest** was a 17 lb. 6 oz. vest with fully armoured front and back for use by bombardiers, navigators, radio operators, waist and tail gunners plus top turret gunners in some aircraft: individuals exposed to injury from the front and back. Pilots and co-pilots[1] wore the 7 lb. 13 oz. **M2 flyer's armour vest**, which had the M1's armour front panel, but its back was unarmoured since pilots were provided armoured seats. Attached to the M1 and M2 vests, by three small snap hooks and 'D' rings, were either the **M3** or **M4 flyer's armour apron**. The 4 lb. 14 oz. M3 was a triangular 'sporran' designed to protect the lower torso and groin areas of those in sitting positions or required to move about in confined spaces. It was worn by pilots and co-pilots, bombardiers and some other crew positions depending on aircraft type. The 7 lb. 2 oz. M4 apron provided more frontal protection with its square shape and was worn by waist gunners and others.

The **M5 flyer's groin armour** was introduced in 1944 to provide even more lower body protection than the M3 and M4 aprons. It was a 15 lb. 4 oz. assembly made up of three sections: the centre section could be drawn between the legs while the thigh sections protected the outer sides of the legs and extended to the knees. It was used by pilots and waist gunners.

In late 1944 a new series of flyer's armour was de-

[1] Officially, bomber pilots were designated aircraft commanders and co-pilots were called pilots.

The S-5 seat parachute was the only type with the wide chest band (on the left side only) supporting the ripcord handle assembly. Its seat cushion is visible. The airman wears an A-10A summer helmet and AN-S-31 summer suit.

B-8 back parachute assembly with the older B-7 harness. Such mixed parachute assemblies were usually interim designs.

veloped. Although of the same basic design as earlier models, the new series were made of hardened aluminium plates and ballistic nylon. They were considerably lighter, e.g. the M6 vest was almost three pounds lighter than the similar M1. The series was standardised on 1 July 1945, but only a small number of M6 vests were issued to Twentieth AF B-29 crews. The **M6** and **M7 flyer's armour vests** were comparable to the M1 and M2 while the **M8** and **M9 flyer's armour aprons** were equivalent to the M3 and M4 aprons. The **M10 flyer's groin armour** was similar to the M5.

A wide range of experimental body armour components were tested, but only one saw wide service use. The **T44 neck armour** was widely field tested in early 1945 and proved effective. The 4.5 lb. 'Queen Anne' T44 was worn in conjunction with the M1 and M2 vests and M4A2 steel helmet. It did restrict vision and head movement somewhat as it was required to be snapped to the helmet. It protected the throat and the head's sides and back.

Steel helmets

Armoured helmets were developed in conjunction with, but as separate components of, body armour. The principal problems with steel helmets were interference with headsets, goggles, and masks: and some turret designs precluded their use due to confined space. Nevertheless, head wounds contributed to a very large percentage of fatal and severe injuries.

Initially, all bomber crewmen were issued standard Hadfield manganese **M1 steel helmets** and **M1 helmet liners,** made of thick, pressed, plastic impregnated duck, as used by ground troops since 1941. These were seldom used as they were almost impossible to wear with headsets and goggles though they were sometimes worn reversed to accommodate goggles). Several unit-initiated attempts were made to modify the M1 helmet to better accommodate these accessories, usually by cutting off the helmet's lip visor to accommodate goggles and/or making semi-circular cutouts in the sides for the headset. A moderately effective method was devised in the autumn of 1943 to spread the helmet and cut out sections of the liner for the headset. Steel helmets were also worn directly over shearling flying helmets without the benefit of the liner; this reduced protection against blunt trauma injury. The need for helmets was critical and British flyers' steel helmets were issued to some bomber crews in 1943. (The following helmets' test designations are included.)

The 3 lb. 3 oz. **M3 steel helmet** (T2) was the first dedicated flyers' steel helmet. Standardised in December 1943, it was a modified M1 with the addition of hinged armoured ear protectors covering the headset cutouts.

In mid-1943 the 'Grow helmet' (named after its designer) was issued to some Eighth AF bomber crews. Modelled after the British flyers' steel helmet, it comprised Hadfield steel plates lined with fabric and covered with dark brown leather. It was a simple dome-shaped helmet with headset cutouts and a leather chin strap assembly. Though the Grow helmet's ear and temple area was exposed, it was standardised on 2 December 1943 as the **M4 steel helmet** (T3) to supplement the M3. It weighed 2 lb. 1 oz. The much improved **M4A1 steel helmet** (T3E3) had hinged steel ear protectors similar to the M3's. Standardised in April 1944, only small numbers of these were made. It was replaced in June 1944 by the more widely issued **M4A2 steel helmet** (M4E2). It was made slightly larger to accommodate more head sizes and better integrate with masks and goggles. The M4A1/A2 helmet bodies and

A B-8 back parachute with a C-2 one-man parachute raft case attached in the seat position, probably a test version. This staff sergeant also wears a B-4 life vest and C-1 emergency vest.

ear protectors were covered with duck and had web chin straps. The improved helmets were authorised for wear by all crewmen of medium, heavy and very heavy bombers, troop carrier transports, and gliders. Fighter pilots seldom, if ever, used steel helmets.

The **M5 flyer's armored helmet** was standardised on 9 March 1945, though a slightly different test version, the **T8 flyer's armoured helmet,** was issued in November 1944. The M3 helmet retained the general profile of the M1, but the M5's size and profile was especially designed for use in confined turrets. However, it could not be worn by A-20 upper turret and B-29 central fire control gunners due to those positions' extreme confinement. The M4A1/A2 and M5 helmets weighed 2 lb. 12 oz. The M1, M3, and M5 were painted dark OD inside and out.

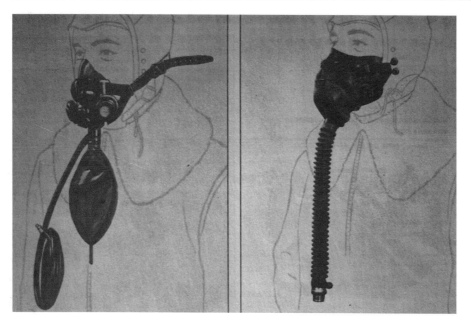

(Left): The A-8B oxygen mask, recognisable by its rebreather bag. This continuous flow mask was extremely prone to freezing and was phased out in 1942. (Right): The A-10 oxygen mask, similar in appearance to the A-9, was made in four variants.

First aid equipment

Several types of crew first aid kits were available aboard aircraft and as a component of some types of E-series survival kits and multiplace life-rafts. Others were intended for individual airmen.

The 1942 **parachute first aid kit No. MD 9710600** ('frying pan insert') was issued with the B-2, -3, and -4 parachute pad emergency kit assemblies (see Emergency Kits). Its small OD painted, circular, flat metal can contained compresses, sufadiazine (anti-infection-'sulfa') tablets and powder, halazone (water purification) tablets, antiseptic, atabrine (anti-malaria) tablets, and boric acid (eyewash).

The **parachute first aid packet No. MD 9778500** was originally issued to paratroopers (often seen fastened to the helmet net), but two were also provided to airmen in 1943 to attach to their parachute harness right shoulder strap for emergency treatment while airborne or after bailout. The 5 oz. waterproofed OD cloth, rubber-lined packet was fitted with two tie tapes and opened by tearing off either end. It contained a field dressing, tourniquet, and morphine syrette.

The **aeronautic first aid kit No. MD 9776500** was standardised in late 1943 by the AAF, US Navy, and British Joint Aeronautic Board. It comprised a two-compartment OD duck container fitted with lift-the-dot snaps to fasten it to matching studs fixed at aircraft crew stations. It was issued on the basis of one kit per two crewmen or one per man at an isolated station. It was also a component of the E-8, -11, and -12 emergency kits. A small snap closed compartment contained adhesive bandaids and iodine swabs to treat minor cuts. The large zipper-closed, double

compartment was sealed and intended to be broken only in case of severe injury. It contained three field dressings, compresses, tourniquet, eye-dressing and burn-injury sets, morphine syrettes, sufadiazine powder or tablets, halazone tablets, and scissors.

The **individual aircrew member first aid packet No. MD 9714000** was available to all airmen, but was principally used by fighter pilots when the aeronautic first aid kit was removed from fighters in early 1945; the latter's components were difficult to use for self aid. The new kit held a field dressing, tape, burn ointment, two morphine syrettes, sufadiazine tablets and powder, halazone tablets, antiseptic, and safety pins, all contained in a 6×4½×1½ in. aluminium box. An improved model, the **A-1 individual aircrew member first aid packet**, was standardised in March 1945.

The 1944 **C-1 flyer's emergency sustenance vest first aid kit** was contained in a small OD plastic box. It held two compresses, four bandaids, burn ointment, two morphine syrettes, and vials of sufadiazine, atabrine, halazone, salt, and benzedrine tablets.

The **life raft first aid kit No. MD 9776900** was issued with the AN-R-2A one-man life raft and multiplace rafts. Packaged in a sealed, waterproofed pasteboard box, its contents were similar to those of the aeronautic first aid kit's, but were not as complete.

The **electric heated casualty bag** was developed by the Eighth AF's Central Medical Establishment in 1943. It was made in the form of a roomy, 'mummy'-type sleeping bag with multiple layers of OD fabric in both 12 and 24 volt versions. Wounded flyers were placed in the bag to protect them from high-altitude cold and to prevent shock. It could also be used to transport a wounded man and in event of ditching at sea, would keep him afloat for 15–20 minutes. Four were carried in heavy bombers. This bag was replaced by the standardised 24 volt **Q-1 electric heated casualty blanket** in 1944. It was of a similar but improved design (including a rubber lining) and would keep a casualty comfortable between 40° and –40°F.

The **electric heated muff** was also developed by the Eighth AF in 12 and 24 volt versions. It was a dark OD cloth-covered affair with internal heating wires; knit wristlets were fitted on both open ends. Five were carried in heavy bombers for use if electric gloves or boots failed; they could be slipped over a foot as well as the hands.

Emergency kits

A number of large type E-series emergency sustenance, or survival, kits were available either for carriage in aircraft for use after a forced landing or for dropping to downed crews when located by search aircraft. Navy issue kits were also used by the AAF. The kits were designed for use in specific areas (arctic, desert, tropic, ocean) and contained rations, canned water, specialised clothing, tools, signal items, medical supplies, and other survival aids. Some even contained an over-and-under .22-cal. rifle/.410 shotgun or .30-cal. M1 carbine. Their size and container styles varied greatly, and the number and type of kits stocked in an aircraft depended on crew size and area of operations. Besides the larger kits, there were several available that could be attached to an airman enabling him to take it with him during bail-out.

The **E-3 emergency sustenance kit** was a personal aids kit standardised on 10 June 1942. It was simply a small plastic box held in an OD cloth bag, secured by a drawstring and small enough to fit in a pocket. It held matches, bouillon powder, chewing gum, malted milk and halazone tablets, 'button' compass, hacksaw blade, and tape.

The **E-6 (rations)** and **E-7 (water) emergency sustenance kits (individual bail-out)** each comprised a small rectangular, two-pocket OD duck pouch with a buckled white web securing strap and snap hook for fastening it to the parachute harness. The E-6 held two K ration meals while the E-7 held two AN-W-5 emergency drinking water cans. Standardised on 27 November 1943, these kits proved not to be of much use and few were procured.

The **E-17 emergency sustenance kit** was another personal aids kit procured from the Military Intelligence Service. It was standardised on 31 July 1944. It was contained in a stout dark OD duck 6×4¼×3in. pouch secured by a flap with two lift-the-dot fasteners; the back was fitted with two web loops plus a belt double hook. Inside were carried an ESM/1 signal mirror and two clear ethyl cellu-

Details of the A-14 oxygen mask retaining strap assembly, shown here along with the A-11 intermediate helmet and B-9 winter jacket.

lose flasks. These had a clip-on lid with a screw-on cap enabling it to be used as a water canteen. One flask contained candy, chewing gum, bouillon powder, matches, fishing hooks and line, 'button' compass, hacksaw blade, razor blades, and condoms (to waterproof small items or carry water). The other flask held a toothbrush, tweezers, tape, bandaids, antiseptics, and six types of medication tablets.

The **E-3A emergency sustenance kit** was a personal aids kit procured from the Military Intelligence Service. It was standardised on 6 April 1945. Of a much different design than the E-3, it was contained in a single flask as used in the E-17 kit. Packed inside were matches, bouillon powder, candy, antiseptic; benzedrine, sulphate, halazone and aspirin tablets, a hacksaw blade, and tape. Though widely issued to airmen as an 'escape' kit, it was of little value and was replaced by the C-1 emergency vest.

Parachute emergency kits replaced standard back or seat pads on parachute harnesses. These 7–8 lb. kits had a pad/container covered with OD duck encasing layers of thick felt with cut-outs for survival items; a zipper ran around the containers' edge. Their contents varied according to area and often changed as the AAF's Arctic, Desert and Tropics Information Center redefined kit specifications. The rations were originally two emergency Air Corps rations, replaced later by two K-ration meals, and still later by emergency parachute rations (see commentary Plate K2).

The **B-1 Alaskan parachute emergency supply kit** was a back pad for seat parachutes, standardised on 7 August 1941. Its contents were meagre compared to other kits' and it was not considered very effective: .45-cal. ball ammo, compass, cooking pan, D-2 gloves[1], fishing tackle, rations, and limited first aid items.

The **B-2** and **B-3 jungle parachute emergency kits** were a back pad for seat parachutes and a seat pad for back parachutes respectively. Their contents were similar: .45-cal. ball and shot ammo, compass, flare kit, fishing tackle, frying pan, first aid kit, medications, rations, D-2 gloves, mosquito headnet, and folding machete. The B-2 was standardised on 16 January 1942 and the B-3 on 12 June 1942.

The much improved **B-4 parachute emergency kit assembly** was a seat or back pad for back and seat parachutes respectively. It was standardised on 7 October 1942 for arctic, desert, and tropical regions. However, it was not issued until late 1943 as earlier kits had to be expended first. Its extensive contents included: .45-cal. shot ammo, compass, collapsible canteen, cooking pan, insert first aid kit, D-2 gloves, H-1 goggles, pocket knife, folding machete, matches, poncho, flare, signal panel, signal mirror, and rations. The limited issue **B-5 parachute emergency kit assembly** was similar, but intended for seat type parachutes and had improved contents. It was standardised on 12 April 1944, but the cases carried the B-4 kit markings.

The parachute emergency kits were replaced by the C-1 vest, on which development began in early 1943. Some units in the Pacific had earlier developed their own survival vests and these influenced the design of the C-1. The parachute kits also often remained in use, usually with their contents modified by their users.

The **C-1 flyer's emergency sustenance vest** was standardised on 3 May 1944, though it saw only limited issue beginning in late 1944. Developed for use in all parts of the world, it was better suited for the tropics than the arctic. Its contents were designed to complement those of the C-2 life raft. The vest was made of dark OD tackle twill and fitted with zippered or snap-closed box pockets. Three large plastic buttons secured the front opening, and it was sized by tie tapes on the back. There were three different size pockets on both sides of the front torso, a smaller pocket on the right front shoulder, three small pockets on the right side, and a duck, leather-lined or all leather pistol holster on the left side. Variants will be found with slightly different pocket arrangements; early vests had the pockets' contents and number printed on them. A 'subdued' or white AAF insignia was printed on the left front shoulder. The pocket layout was designed to allow the vest to be worn under the parachute harness and life vest. The vest was also carried in a modified M1936 field bag (musette

bag) attached to the left side of a parachute harness. The 11 lb. vest contained: .45-cal. shot ammo, fire starting kit, first aid kit, fishing/sewing kit, gloves and inserts, H-1 goggle, reversible hat (yellow/OD), mosquito headnet, insect repellent, pocket knife, sharpening stone, two emergency parachute rations, two signal flares, ESM/1 or 2 signal mirror, spit and gaff assembly, M1943 collapsible canteen, collapsible asbestos cooking utensil, and other small survival aids.

Life vests and rafts

The **B-3** and **B-4 pneumatic life preserver vests**, almost identical in design, were commonly known as the 'Mae West'. They were of the horse-collar style designed to keep a man's head above water even if unconscious; they could not keep a man in full flying clothes afloat, however. Web waist and crotch straps secured the vest to the wearer. The B-3, standardised on 8 January 1938, had double compartments made of cotton fabric encasing two separate latex rubber bladders. The Navy-designed AN-V-18 vest was standardised by the Army as the B-4 on 6 May 1942. It had two superimposed compartments constructed from rubber-coated fabric; it was stiffer and less comfortable than the B-3, but simpler to manufacture and used less rubber, now a scarce commodity. The B-4 was redesignated the AN6519–1 vest on 1 February 1944. Navy AN-V-18 vests were also used by the AAF. All variations had orange-yellow casings and straps and were inflated by two pull-cord activated 0.280 oz. CO_2 cylinders near the bottom ends, or by a pair of oral inflation tubes on the right upper front.

The AAF-designed **B-5 pneumatic life preserver vest** was standardised on 12 December 1944 to replace the B-3/B-4, although they remained in use (the B-5 is still standard). Similar in appearance to the earlier types, it was

The M1 armour vest and M3 armour apron; the quick release strap on the midriff is red and the connecting webbing is white. An M4 steel, or 'Grow', helmet is worn over a shearling flying helmet.

[1] The D-2 mechanics' gloves are described in USAAF Book 2.

of considerably different construction. It allowed the head to float up higher out of the water and kept the wearer more vertical, regardless of weight. It also had improved retaining strap and inflation systems. It weighed 3 lbs., the B-3/B-4 weighed four. Two snap-closed pockets were fitted between the flotation chambers for survival aids.

Life jacket dye markers (yellow-green fluorscein dye) were often attached to the life vest's left side by tie cords or rubber cement. These were approximately 5×5 in. packets opened by pull-tabs; there were several versions, all made of the same material as life jackets. **Life vest shark deterrent packets** held a cake of so-called 'shark chaser'. The blue waterproof packet was torn open and the cake swished in the water making a blue-black cloud, which also doubled as a dye marker. The cake was attached to the packet by a tape and could be returned to the packet for reuse. They were attached to the right side of life vests between the chambers. The Navy issue **life jacket attachable light** was provided to AAF airmen. It was a small, single-battery, grey or orange plastic flashlight fitted with a safety pin for attachment to clothing.

Several four-man (types A-2, -3, -3A) and six-man (types E-1, -2, -2A) inflatable rubber life rafts were part of the on-board equipment supplied with bombers and transports, fitted in wing and upper fuselage pop-out compartments. A considerable amount of survival equipment and supplies were packed in these rafts. The only rafts we will discuss here are the one-man type that could be attached to parachute harnesses as an uncomfortable seat cushion. All models were packed in OD duck parachute pack cases. Small experimental rafts (B-1 and C-1) were tested prior to the war, but were not adopted due to bulk problems and storage space in fighters.

The **AN-R-2** and **AN-R-2A (AN6520–1) one-man parachute rafts** were used by fighter pilots and bomber crews flying overwater routes. This 66 in. long, 40 in. wide (inflated) raft was made of two-ply orange-yellow rubberised fabric. It was inflated by a ¾ lb. CO_2 cylinder, but also had an oral inflation tube. The 16 lb. raft and pack case contained a can of drinking water, paulin sheet (reversible blue/yellow and used for shade, weather protection, signalling, camouflage, catching rain water), sea anchor, bailing cup, hand paddles, raft first aid kit, raft repair kit, orange-yellow sail, and sea marker dye. The AN-R-2 was standardised by the AAF on 4 July 1942. The differences between the two models was the case. The Navy-designed AN-R-2 case had a slot in the centre for the parachute har-

ness's leg straps. This did not fit AAF harnesses well and the AN-R-2A case, standardised on 20 August 1942, eliminated the slot.

The AN-R-2A was replaced by the similar **C-2 one-man parachute raft** standardised on 21 April 1944, although the former remained in use. The C-2 was slightly smaller and included the addition of a blue spray shield, new-type sail and collapsible mast, and an improved case totalling 22 lbs. The case was fitted with a 1 in. wide web static line that attached to the right side of the harness. The case could be released while the jumper was still airborne, automatically inflating the raft enabling him to board it immediately after landing. Its accessories were essentially the same as the AN-R-2A's, but with the addition of an MX-137/A radar reflector, AN-CPT-2 radar beacon, M75 flares, ESM/1 signal mirrors, JJ-1 sea water desalting kit, and hand pump. The first aid kit was deleted, one being available in the C-1 emergency vest. The slightly improved **C-2A one-man parachute raft** was standardised on 21 May 1945.

* * *

A fully outfitted B-17 waist gunner wears a flak suit comprising the M1 vest and M4 apron. He wears the AN-H-16 winter helmet, A-14 oxygen mask (connected to an extension hose), and A-6 winter shoes.

A common complaint of flyers, particularly bomber crewmen, was that they felt like a Christmas tree when fully outfitted with layers of heavy clothing, electric heated suit, gloves, shoes, flying helmet, goggle, headset, oxygen mask, walk around and bail-out bottles, pistol, emergency kit or vest, life vest, life raft, parachute, steel helmet, and flak suit. All of this weighed close to 100 lbs.—a heavy load to bear in cramped quarters and fatigue-inducing cold while flying a plane or working its guns.

THE PLATES

A1: Fighter pilot, 77th Pursuit Squadron; USA, 1941
This newly commissioned 2nd lieutenant was one of thousands of pilots turned out by the Flying Training Command during the AAF's massive expansion. The 77th Pursuit Squadron (Interceptor) was then equipped with P-39 Airacobras and based at Hamilton Field, Calif.; its famous 'poker hand' insignia dates from 1931. All 'pursuit' squadrons were redesignated 'fighter' on 15 May 1942. This fledgling pilot wears the A-8 summer helmet with a T-30 throat microphone, B-7 goggles, A-2 jacket with 'leather insignia' and name plate, A-4 summer suit, B-2 summer gloves, and 'moccasin' style B-5 winter shoes. This ensemble is worn over the standard officer's wool OD shirt and trousers. Black neckties were replaced by dark OD in February 1942, but continued to be issued until supplies were exhausted. Prior to August 1942 officers' rank were worn on the shirt's shoulder straps with the U.S. device and branch of service insignia on the collars.

A2 and A3: Bomber crewmen, 40th Bombardment Squadron; USA, 1941
These B-18A Bolo bomber crewmen are outfitted in the winter B-3 jacket and A-3 trousers adopted in 1934. War-time production jackets were often of 'two-tone' construction with some of the panels (sleeve shoulders and undersides, cuff and waist bands, pocket) in dark brown rather than the much darker seal brown. Both wear A-8 winter gloves and A-6 winter shoes. Figure *A2* also wears the B-5 winter helmet and B-7 goggle assembly and is trying the fit of an A-7 nasal oxygen mask. The unusual A-7 mask was also used with some early walk-around assemblies. His parachute is contained in the A-3 flyer's kit bag at his feet. Figure *A3* wears the enlisted man's garrison cap adorned with Air Forces ultramarine blue and golden orange branch of service piping. Units authorised a distinctive unit insignia (crest)[1] would wear it in place of the officer's Air Forces branch of service insignia worn here. He is outfitted with the B-7 back parachute. The A-2 and -3 QAC and S-1 seat types' harnesses were similar.

A4: General Headquarters Air Force shoulder sleeve insignia
The GHQAF was formed on 1 March 1935 as the Air Corps' first air force and was responsible for the control of heavy bombardment units. The stylised 'impeller blades' represented its three original bombardment wings. When the AAF was formed on 20 June 1941, the GHQAF was redesignated the Air Force Combat Command and was now responsible for the four continental air forces' bomber and fighter commands. Another reorganisation saw the command redesignated Headquarters Squadron of the AAF on 8 March 1942. This patch was approved on 20 July 1937 and was retained through its redesignations until the AAF patch was approved (Plate E4). Organisational patches were worn ½ in. below the left shoulder seam.

B1 and B2: Bomber crewmen, 340th Bombardment Squadron; EIO, 1942
B-17E Flying Fortress crews flying their first missions out of England in August 1942 were ill-equipped with flying clothes. This resulted in a high percentage of cold injuries, increased crew fatigue, and much discomfort and inefficiency due to bulkiness. A typical airman was equipped with the winter B-6 jacket and A-5 trousers, B-6 winter helmet, flying type all purpose goggles, A-10 winter gloves, and A-6 winter shoes. Electric heated items, as worn by Figure *B2*, were also issued including the F-1 suit, E-1 gloves, and D-1 shoes. Figure *B1* is testing the fit of his B-8A oxygen mask; the rebreather bag was highly prone to freezing; he holds an oxygen mask container, and an H-1 emergency oxygen assembly (bail-out bottle) is strapped to his leg. Slung over his shoulder is a high-pressure continuous flow walk-around assembly. Figure *B2* wears the popular B-2

A 36th Troop Carrier Squadron C-47 flight engineer displays the M1 armour vest and M3 apron he wore during Operation 'Market Garden': a single 7.92mm bullet struck at point No. 4, and the other points indicate where bullet fragments struck. This photo is part of the series distributed to airmen in an effort to convince them to wear the heavy flak suits.

[1] Groups and higher units were authorised crests, which were worn by subordinate squadrons. The authorisation of crests was ceased in 1943 to conserve materials.

winter flying cap. Beside him is an A-1 food container (aircraft) holding four 1 qt. class A type 1 vacuum bottles of coffee; sandwiches were held in the food compartment. Crews were warned that vacuum bottles filled with boiling beverages should not be opened within three hours at 20,000 ft. or six hours at 30,000 ft.—because of the reduced air pressure, the contents would well exceed the boiling point. The 340th Bombardment Squadron (Heavy) was one of the first US units to operate out of England.

B3: Eighth Air Force shoulder sleeve insignia

The 'Mighty Eighth' was formed at Savannah, Ga., on 28 January 1942 and soon began deploying to England. The patch (*3a*), made in England, was originally intended for VIII Bomber Command, which arrived in England in April 1942. When Maj.Gen. Carl Spaatz arrived in England in June, activating the 8th AF there, he accepted the VIII Bomber Command patch for the 8th AF[1]. On 25 March 1943 the War Department notified field commanders to submit shoulder sleeve insignia designs to the Quartermaster General for approval. The design (*3b*), approved on 20 May 1943, displayed different style wings.

B4: Bomber crewman, 77th Bombardment Squadron; Aleutians, 1942

This B-26 Marauder crewman is protected against the brutal –40°F encountered in Alaska's Aleutian Islands. The operating conditions were so harsh in the Aleutians that the 77th Bombardment Squadron (Medium), the first B-26 unit committed to combat, lost 18 aircraft to weather and mechanical failure alone in the first year. He is outfitted in the winter B-7 jacket and A-6 trousers, B-2 winter cap, amber Polaroid flying goggles, A-9 winter gloves, and A-10 winter shoes. Medium bomber and fighter pilots operating in other parts of the world generally used lighter ensembles than worn by heavy bomber crews: usually wool or cotton service uniforms worn with or without flying suits and accompanied by an appropriate weight flying jacket. Of course, in winter conditions, full shearling or alpaca flying suits would be donned.

B5: Eleventh Air Force shoulder sleeve insignia

The Alaskan AF was formed 15 January 1942 at Elmendorf Field. On 5 February it was redesignated the 11th AF. Its patch was approved on 13 August 1943.

C1: Transport pilot, 42nd Transport Squadron; Alaska, 1942

This member of the first C-47 Skytrain unit to deploy to Alaska wears the winter B-7 jacket and A-8 trousers, B-6

B-17 waist gunner outfitted with the M3 steel helmet, M1 armour vest, and three-piece M5 groin armour.

winter helmet, A-11 winter gloves, and A-12 winter shoes. The B-7/A-6 suit was insulated with mixed chicken feathers and down. He carries an over-and-under .22-cal. rifle/ .410 shotgun issued in the types E-2, -8, -10, -12, and -14 emergency sustenance kits, though replaced by the .30-cal. M1 carbine in some late manufacture kits. Beside him is an arctic first aid kit; this, and the similar jungle version, were issued to heavy and medium bomber and transport crews overflying those areas. The Elmendorf Field-based 42nd Transport flew supplies to far-flung American posts throughout Alaska. Transport squadrons were redesignated troop carrier on 4 July 1942.

C2: Ferry pilot, North Atlantic Wing, 1943

The winter B-11 jacket and A-10 trousers were externally similar to the feather and down insulated B-8/A-9 suit, but alpaca-lined. Under the suit is a knit shirt, a long-sleeve sweater, worn over the wool service uniform for maximum protection on the brutal US-Canada-Greenland-Iceland-United Kingdom transatlantic route. This captain wears his service cap with the crown stiffener spring removed to obtain the '50 mission crush' look; more practically, this allowed a radio/intercom HS-38 headset to be worn. Wearing A-7 winter shoes (inserts), he has not yet donned his A-6 winter shoes. He wears an A-7 wrist-watch standardised in 1934.

[1] On 18 September 1942 air force designations were changed from Arabic numbers to fully spelled out, e.g. the 8th AF became the Eighth.

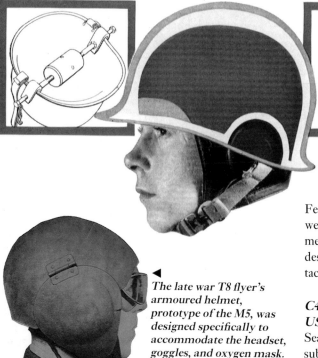

This modification of the M1 steel helmet and liner, developed in the autumn of 1943, allowed the radio headset to be worn comfortably. A screw-jack was used to spread the steel helmet and the helmet liner's 'ear' sections were cut out. Leather flying helmets with earphones were then attached to the steel helmet's web suspension.

◄ *The late war T8 flyer's armoured helmet, prototype of the M5, was designed specifically to accommodate the headset, goggles, and oxygen mask. The M5 had welded hinges and was made of manganese steel rather than the T8's Swedish steel.*

C3: Air Forces Transport Command shoulder sleeve insignia

Several versions of this patch exist, reflecting the command's redesignations. The red-white-blue markings around the edge represent Morse code 'dits and dahs' and can be found reading 'ACFC'—Air Corps Ferrying Command (May 1941 to May 1942); 'AFFO'—Air Forces Ferrying Command (to June 1942); and 'AFATC'—Air Forces Air Transport Command (to July 1945). The gold-yellow backed patch (*3a*) was used by the first two commands and the silver-grey one (*3b*) by the AFATC, though earlier examples often remained in use. The insignia was painted on all the command's aircraft, and larger 'squadron-size' patches were made for flying jackets, along with metal crests for uniforms. The ACFC/AFFC was responsible for delivery of aircraft from factories to units in the States as well as to overseas units and Allies. It was also assigned duties beyond this due to wartime necessity such as cargo transport and operating overseas air routes. It was organised into regionally oriented wings. The Air Service Command (ASC) was also responsible for air transport within the US, while the 'old' Air Transport Command took care of tactical transport including parachute and glider operations, causing much duplication of effort. The Ferrying Command and air transport elements of the ASC were merged in June 1942 as the AFATC, to handle all domestic and theatre air transport. The 'old' ATC was redesignated the Troop Carrier Command, responsible for tactical operations.

C4: Bomber crewman, 3rd Search Attack Squadron; USA, 1943

Search attack units, along with the more numerous anti-submarine squadrons, operated principally under the First AF's I Bomber Command to hunt down U-boats off the US East Coast. Initially, all available bombers, attack, and recce aircraft were employed, but the radar-equipped B-18A and B-24 Liberator later became the real sub-hunter workhorses. In October 1942 I Bomber Command was redesignated the Antisubmarine Command. Its 25 squadrons, along with Navy aviation squadrons, virtually eliminated the coastal U-boat threat. In August 1943 the command reverted to its former designation and mission with the antisubmarine role turned over to the Navy, though AAF units still provided assistance. The last of the shearling flying suits to be developed, the winter AN-J-4 jacket and AN-T-35 trousers, remained in use to the war's end, but only in the States. He wears an A-11 intermediate helmet, A-11 winter gloves, and A-6 winter shoes. To help endure the long, cold, lone aircraft patrols, a 2 gal. thermos container of coffee will be loaded; a similar 1 gal. version was also used. He inspects a 37mm AN-M8 flare pistol carried on all bombers and transports and also issued in the E-11 and -15 emergency kits. The AN-M8 was adopted in early 1943 and came with an A-2 holster and A-5, -6, or -7 cartridge containers, all made of OD duck.

D1: Fighter pilot, 99th Fighter Squadron; Italy, 1944

This P-51 Mustang pilot wears the new intermediate B-10 jacket and A-9 trousers. This early version has shoulder straps and dark brown knit wristlets and waist band. A plastic police whistle is attached to collar, a common practice, to signal rescue boats if down in the water. Under the jacket he wears a C–2 winter vest over his wool service uniform. From August 1942 the U.S. device, formerly worn on the right shirt collar, was replaced with rank, until then, worn on shoulder straps. While many bomber pilots wore neckties, to emphasize their businesslike, behind-the-front-desk job, the more flamboyant fighter pilots dispensed with the tie to allow greater freedom to scan the sky. He also wears the A–11 intermediate helmet, B–7 goggles, and A–11 wrist-watch, standardised in 1940. He wears the overseas rough side out leather service shoes with plain toes. The all African-American 99th, 100th, 301st, and 302nd Fighter Squadrons never lost a bomber they escorted. They were known as the 'Tuskegee Airmen', their primary training being conducted at Tuskegee Institute in Alabama; or as the 'Red Tails', after their fighters' tail fin colour, they served as part of the 332nd Fighter and later the 477th Composite Groups. The 477th also included the 616th–619th Bombardment Squadrons with B–25s.

D2: Bomber crewman, 514th Bombardment Squadron; Italy, 1944

The F–2 electric heated suit comprised a simple outer jacket and trousers worn over electric jacket and trouser inserts. The F–1 electric heated felt shoe inserts were designed to be worn inside A–6 shoes. These inserts were also worn with the F–3/F–3A electric suit. The F–2 electric gloves (see Plate D3) were also worn with this outfit. The AN6505–1 aviator's kit bag replaced the old A–3 flyer's bag. Based in Italy, the Fifteenth AF's B–24 units flew many missions into Germany in co-ordination with the Eighth AF launching out of England.

D3: Bomber crewman, 736th Bombardment Squadron; ETO, 1944

The improvements made in clothing available to airmen were reflected in items issued to replacement bomber crews from January 1944: intermediate B–10 jacket and A–9 trousers (here, the late, dark OD version), A–4 summer suit, F–2 electric suit, B–6 or AN-H–16 winter helmet (the latter is worn here), A–11 or A–9 winter gloves, A–12 arctic gloves, F–2 electric gloves (worn here), rayon glove inserts, A–6A winter shoes, and F–1 electric shoe inserts. Waist gunners were additionally issued the winter B–11 jacket and A–10 trousers, while ball turret gunners were equipped with F–2 electric felt shoes. This B–17F radio operator, manning a 65 lb., upward firing .50-cal. M2 flexible machine gun (with a 100-round ammo container), is also outfitted with the B–8 goggles (issued in kit form with

interchangeable clear, green, and amber lenses), A–10R oxygen mask attached to an extension hose, H–2 emergency oxygen assembly, and A–4 QAC parachute harness (chest pack removed). The B–9 back and S–5 seat types' harnesses were similar in design. A flak suit would be worn over all this. On the floor is a low-pressure continuous flow walk-around bottle.

D4: Mediterranean Theatre of Operations air forces' shoulder sleeve insignia

Three air forces deployed to the MTO during the war's course. (4a) The Ninth AF was formed from the 5th Air Support Command on 8 April 1942 at New Orleans Army Air Base, La. Its advance elements deployed to Egypt in June as the US Army Middle East AF. Its main elements arrived in November to conduct missions throughout the eastern Mediterranean, Italy, and the Balkans. In October 1943 it deployed to England and reorganised as a tactical air force to support ground forces after the invasion. Its patch was approved on 16 September 1943. (4b) The Twelfth AF was formed at Bolling Field, DC, on 20 August 1942, deployed to England, and supported the North African landings in November. It operated from Tunisia throughout North Africa, Sicily, Italy, and Southern France. The patch was approved on 1 December 1943. (4c) The Fifteenth AF was formed from the Twelfth's XII Bomber Command in Tunis, Tunisia, on 1 November 1943. The next month it moved to Italy from where it flew missions into Germany and the Balkans. Its patch was approved on 19 February 1944.

E1: Recce Pilot, 14th Photographic Reconnaissance Squadron; ETO, 1944

The intermediate B–15 jacket and A–11 trousers were to remain the standard flying suit through the remainder of the war. An AAF patch is printed on the left shoulder. This F–5 pilot wears the AN-H–16 winter helmet, A–11A winter gloves, and A–6A winter shoes. Fighter type recce aircraft had heated cockpits, eliminating the need for electric suits.

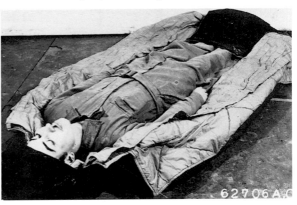

The Eighth AF developed electric heated casualty bag. The bag is open, but can be closed and secured by tie-tapes. Four were carried in heavy bombers.

He holds an aeronautic first aid kit provided in all aircraft. The A-13 oxygen mask was of the pressure-demand type permitting ascent above 40,000 ft., a necessity for the extremely high altitudes required for recce missions. There were a wide range of different types of recce squadrons, which went through a bewildering series of redesignations. They were equipped with recce variants of standard aircraft, fitted with cameras and extra fuel tanks and with most armour and guns removed: F-3 (A-20A), F-4 and -5 (P-38E), F-6 (P-51), F-7 (B-24J), F-9 (B-17F), F-10 (B-25D), and F-13 (B-29A). Recce units provided both pre- and post-strike recce, conducted aerial mapping, and supported ground forces with tactical reconnaissance.

E2: Bomber crewman, 748th Bombardment Squadron; ETO, 1944

The two-piece F-3 electric heated suit was designed to integrate with the A-15/A-11 suit. Q-1 electric heated shoe inserts were worn over standard service shoes and inside A-6A winter shoes. F-2 electric gloves completed the ensemble. The popular highneck sweater is worn over the wool service uniform and wool long underwear. An FTG-3 food storage container (also called a Tappan B-2 food warmer) was authorised on the basis of two per very heavy and heavy bombers and one per six men, or fraction thereof, on smaller bombers, though intended for B-29s. It held 12 1 pt. cups and six four-compartment trays in their own heated compartments, and had a drawer for sandwiches, condiments, and utensils. The warmer was plugged into the aircraft's power system as used for the electric suits. The B-2 was not too successful due to cleaning problems, and the reheated food was considered unpalatable; crews preferred simple sandwiches and coffee.

E3: Bomber crewman, 335th Bombardment Squadron; ETO, 1945

In late 1944 combat units received a massive replenishment of clothing stocks, which rendered inadequate clothing a

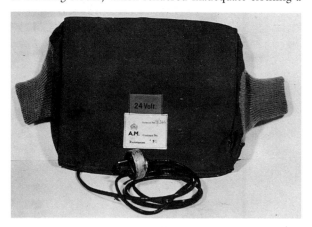

negligible factor in causing frostbite. The intermediate B-15A/A-11A suit, worn over an F-3A electric suit, offered a number of refinements over the A-15/A-11. The AN-H-16 winter helmet, B-8 goggle, and A-14 oxygen mask comprise the head assembly. The mask's hose is attached to an AN6020-1 low-pressure demand walk-around unit, clipped to a tab; it is also attached to an H-2 emergency oxygen assembly. F-2 electric gloves and F-2 electric heated felt shoes complete the protective clothing. An AN6519-1 life vest (same as a B-4), with a sea dye marker packet, is worn under a B-10 back parachute harness. The A-5 QAC and S-6 seat type harnesses were similar. A parachute first aid kit is strapped to the harness. This navigator double checks his calculations on an E-6B aerial dead reckoning computer.

E4: Army Air Forces shoulder sleeve insignia

(4a) This patch was approved on 19 March 1942 for wear by all AAF units and organisations. Gradually, numbered air forces and some other organisations replaced it with their own designs. It was retained by all those not authorised a designated insignia. (4b) The comparatively rare reversed colour AAF patch appears to be a semi-official variant worn on both OD and khaki uniforms at the individual's discretion.

F1: Bomber bail-out, 1943

This B-17E crewman is exiting from the tail gunner's emergency hatch. He wears an A-2 QAC parachute displaying the back pad and an AN-R-2A one-man raft parachute pack case. All emergency parachutes were manually activated by pulling a ripcord. Airmen were advised to delay their opening for two to six seconds to ensure they cleared the aircraft; this also served to slow their falling speed, thus reducing opening shock. From high altitudes, airmen were advised to freefall to a lower altitude before opening. This sped the airman's descent through the intense cold and rarified air at high altitudes, even though he might possess a bail-out bottle and protective clothing; a long parachute ride at high altitudes could be debilitating or even fatal. It was also safer to freefall through a layered bomber formation, and effectively prevented attack by enemy aircraft. In 1944 an automatic opening device was developed for the A-3 QAC parachute and saw limited use. This device's aneroid-activated switch automatically opened the parachute at a pre-set altitude in the event of the airman being disabled.

The Eighth AF developed 24 volt electric heated muff. The British Air Ministry contract tag is affixed under the 24 volt identification tag. Five of these were required to be carried in heavy bombers.

F2: Water landing, 1944

The B-3, -4 (worn here), and -5 life preserver vests were worn under the parachute harness, here a B-8 back type, which had to be shed prior to activating the CO_2 cylinders or the wearer's chest would be crushed. Besides the obvious hazards of a water landing, a major concern was entanglement in suspension lines and/or canopy. Airmen were instructed to release their harness fastenings prior to landing, keeping their arms tucked into the sides to prevent falling out, and throwing them upward when hitting the drink. The jumper would then slide out the harness and swim upwind or up current away from the discarded parachute.

F3: Fighter bail-out, 1945

Fighter pilots, in these pre-ejection seat days, would attempt to turn the aircraft over, jettison the canopy, release the lap belt and shoulder harness, and kick themselves out. Oxygen mask hose and headset wires would disconnect if the pilot failed to do it. In combat, this form of bail-out was a relative luxury. This P-51 pilot wears a B-5 seat parachute with its seat cushion. A C-1 emergency vest is carried in a modified (with strap, snap hook, 'V' ring added to its back) M1936 field bag attached to the harness.

G1: Developmental flyer's body armor, 1943

The first flak jackets issued were the contract, British-made prototypes. Here, the fully armored Type A full vest and Type C tapered apron are worn. These were soon redesignated the T1 and T3, being standardised as the M1 and M3 respectively in October 1943. The Type B half vest had an unarmored back for wear by pilots and the Type D apron was of a square design. These were redesignated the T2 and T4 and standardised as the M2 and M4. The M3 steel helmet was a modified M1 with ear protectors and headset cut-outs.

G2: Issue flyer's body armor, 1944

This gunner wears the standardised M1 full vest and M4 square apron. He also wears the leather covered M4 steel, or 'Grow', helmet modeled after the British version. The red web pull strap activates the quick release system.

G3: Issue flyer's body armor, 1945

This B-29A Superfortress pilot is outfitted for high altitude operations in the M2 half vest and M5 groin armor, a three-piece assembly providing increased protection. The M5 steel helmet was similar to the earlier T-8. He also wears the AN6530 goggles (same as B-8), A-14 oxygen mask, H-2 bail-out bottle, B-15A/A-11A suit, and A-11A gloves. He is secured in his armored seat by a B-14 lap safety belt and B-15 safety shoulder harness. These were

A staff sergeant demonstrates the vest type emergency kit, the experimental predecessor of the C-1 flyer's emergency sustenance vest. This test version had small tubular pockets at the front opening and collar. He sits on an S-1 seat parachute and C-2 one-man raft case.

standardised in 1944 to replace the B-11 lap belt and various shoulder harnesses in all fighter, bomber, and transport pilot's and co-pilot's seats.

G4: Modified flyer's steel helmet, 1944

Though replaced by improved designs, unit-modified M1 steel helmets remained in use. Occasionally, an airman would personalise his helmet; this one was used by a B-26 tail gunner in the 323rd Bombardment Group. Mission number and target name were pencilled on the bombs.

G5: Issue flyer's steel helmet, 1944

The M4A2 steel helmet was one of the most widely worn flyers' armoured helmets. The M4A1 helmet was of identical design, but the A2 was made slightly larger. All models were worn over shearling flying helmets and were designed to integrate with headsets, goggles, and oxygen masks.

H1: Fighter pilot, 44th Fighter Squadron; Pacific, 1943

The A-4 summer suit was the standard flying suit until replaced by the AN-S-3 and -31. This P-40 Warhawk pilot on Guadalcanal wears the A-8 summer helmet, B-7 goggles, and B-2 summer gloves. To accompany him on his mission he has a sack lunch, 1 qt. M1910 water canteen, and 1 pt. class B type 1 vacuum bottle of coffee (also available in 1 and 2 qt. capacities). He carries a .38-cal. S&W Victory Model revolver in a Navy issue shoulder holster traded from a Marine aviator.

H2: Fighter pilot, 402nd Fighter Squadron; ETO, 1944

The AN-S-31 summer suit was intended to replace the A-4, but the older suit remained in use through the war. Worn over the AN-S-31 is the Clark G-3 fighter pilot's pneumatic, or anti-G, suit. The later G-3A was based on this suit rather than the Berger G-3. This P-38 Lightning pilot carries the anti-G suit's carrying case and wears B-3 summer gloves. The AN-H-15 summer helmet proved to be unsatisfactory and was replaced by the similar A-10A. He is also outfitted with two British-made items used by many UK-based fighter pilots throughout the war: the Mk IV goggles (with the flip-down anti-glare lens removed) and a dull yellow Mk I life jacket.

H3: Bomber crewman, 8th Bombardment Squadron; Pacific, 1944

This B-25 Mitchell crewman, operating out of New Guinea to attack Rabaul, is outfitted in the L-1 light suit, A-10A summer helmet, B-8 goggles, and B-3A summer gloves. The K-1 very light suit was of the same design but made of khaki Byrd cloth. He carries a leather organisation equipment list container holding his aircraft's extensive roster of on-board gear.

H4: Asiatic-Pacific Theater of Operations air forces' shoulder sleeve insignia

Five air forces operated in the Pacific and Asia. (4a) Ori-

ginally formed as the Philippine Department AF on 20 September 1941, the 5th AF was activated on Java on 5 February 1942. It fought throughout the Southwest Pacific and later moved to Okinawa to attack Japan. Its patch was approved on 25 March 1943. (4b) The 10th AF was activated at Patterson Field, Ohio, on 12 February 1942 and moved to India. It operated in Burma and China, later moving up to that front. The patch was approved on 25 January 1944. (4c) The Thirteenth AF was formed on New Caledonia on 13 January 1943 to operate in the Central and Southwest Pacific. Its patch was approved on 18 January, 1944. (4d) The Fourteenth AF was formed from the China Air Task Force (formed in mid-1942) on 10 March 1943 at Kunming, China. It flew operations from Burma to Japan. The patch was approved on 6 August 1943 reflecting its origins in the old 'Flying Tigers'. (4e) The Twentieth AF was activated at Washington, DC, on 4 April 1944. Equipped solely with B-29s, its mission was to bomb Japan into submission. Elements first launched out of China, but later the entire force operated from Pacific islands. Its patch was approved on 26 May 1944.

I1: Fighter pilot, 1st Fighter Squadron (Commando); Asia, 1944

The Tenth AF's 1st and 2nd Air Commando Groups included some of the more nondescript flyers in a branch that tended to foster non-adherence to uniform regulations. This P-51 pilot wears a self-camouflaged AN-S-3 summer suit, Australian bush hat, D-1 goggles, A-11 wrist-watch, and Wellington boots. Even his M7 shoulder holster, with a pearl-handled .45-cal. M1911A1 pistol, is worn as a belt holster. He is placing one of the flasks of the E-17 personal aids kit in his pocket.

I2: Flying jacket art

The artwork painted on the backs of flying jackets, especially the A-2, whether utilitarian or fanciful, depicted squadron insignia, boastful victory slogans, scantily clad pinups inspired by movie goddesses (Glory Girls), duplications of aircraft nose art, and threats of vengeance to be inflicted on the enemy. Headquarters sometimes attempted to 'clean up' the usually nude ladies on which nose art often focused, but the crews who complied only added negligées or G-strings. (2a) The approved insignia of the 90th Bombardment Group (Heavy) 'Jolly Rogers' was repeated on the tails of its B-24s. He also wears a B-1 summer

The orange-yellow B-4 pneumatic life preserver vest with shark deterrent and dye marker packets attached. An opened blue *'shark chaser' packet is to the left of the vest. The B-3 and AN6519-1 vests were identical in appearance.*

cap and flying sun glasses (comfort cable type). (*2b*) The 'Wild Children' of a 390th Bombardment Group (Heavy) B-17 crew display their bomber's nose art along with their completed missions and kills. (*2c*) 'Dark Lady' replicated the nose art of a P-61 Black Widow night fighter in the VII Fighter Command. He wears the E-1 dark adaptation goggles[1].

J1: Anti-exposure suit, 1944

The R-1 quick-donning anti-exposure suit kept the flyer dry and afloat, but relied on flying clothes worn underneath to provide the necessary insulation from frigid waters. The hood and boots were integral, but the one-finger F-1 exposure gloves were stowed in the pockets. He also wears a water-resistant helmet supplied in the E-11 emergency kit. He has ignited a Mk 1 Mod 1 distress smoke hand signal.

J2: B-4 life preserver, 1943

This B-4 life preserver vest (B-3 and AN6519-1 were externally identical) has dye marker and shark deterrent packets attached to it. It was common for the life vest technical order number, inspection dates, and the crewman's name to be stencilled on the front panel. This airman wears a water-resistant helmet, found in some emergency kits, and a wartime production 'two-tone' B-3 winter jacket. He holds an A-9 hand energised flashlight, a component of multiplace life rafts.

J3: B-5 life preserver, 1945

The later B-5 life preserver vest offered pockets for a Navy attachable light (pinned to his shoulder), plastic police whistle, and dye marker; an ESM/1 signal mirror and shark deterrent packet could be added. He holds an AN6522-1 emergency fishing kit container, which could be donned as a chest apron. He wears a B-1 summer cap, K-1 very light suit, and K-1 mosquito-resistant very light gloves.

J4: C-1 emergency vest, 1944

The C-1 flyer's emergency sustenance vest contained a surprising quantity of survival aids. A .45-cal. M1911A1 pistol is held in its integral holster. He wears an emergency reversible sun hat and H-1 eye protective goggles, both components of the vest. He also wears an A-9 summer suit, rayon glove inserts, and holds an M75 handheld, two-star signal flare, a component of the C-2 one-man raft.

J5: Emergency radio transmitter

The AN/CRT-3 radio, known as a 'Gibson Girl' due to its shape, was the last model issued; the others were the very

This technical sergeant models an inflated B-5 life preserver vest revealing its improved retaining strap system and accessory pockets containing an attachable light, police whistle, and dye marker.

similar SCR-578A and B. These were provided in multiplace life rafts and packed in a container with two ballons, chemical hydrogen generators, a kite (to hoist the antenna wire aloft) and accessories. The 9×11×12 in., 34–38 lb. radios had a 50–300 mile range.

K1: Walk-around and bail-out oxygen assemblies

Portable (walk-around) and emergency (bail-out) oxygen bottles were crucial gear for airmen operating above 10,000 ft. See the Oxygen Cylinder Assemblies section for details. A 12 in. ruler is provided for scale. (*1a*) High-pressure continuous flow walk-around assembly. (*1b*) Low-pressure continuous flow walk-around assembly. (*1c*) Low-pressure demand walk-around assembly. (*1d*) AN6020-1 low-pressure demand walk-around unit. (*1e*) Regulator and cylinder assembly-diluter demand oxygen. (*1f*) H-1 emergency

[1] 'Dark Lady' jacket information provided courtesy of Robert G. Borrell, Sr.

oxygen cylinder assembly. (*1g*) H-2 emergency oxygen cylinder assembly.

K2: In-flight and emergency rations

A number of special rations were available to airmen for in-flight meals and survival situations. (*2a*) The 1934 *emergency air corps ration* had three 4 oz. enriched chocolate cakes in a key-opened, galvanised container, which could be used to hold water. It was originally issued as part of B-1, -2, and -3 parachute emergency kits, but was later replaced by (2f), and still later by (2g). For individual issue it was superseded by (2b), but still issued into 1944. (*2b*) The *type D field ration* had three 4 oz. vitamin-enriched, tropical chocolate bars (would not melt in high temperatures) in a pasteboard carton. A bar could be boiled in a canteen cup of water to make cocoa. Fighter pilots were often issued one D ration per mission. (*2c*) Seven units of 1945 *type A life raft rations* were provided as a component of multiplace rafts. Its key-opened can held 12 packages of Charms candy, 18 pieces chewing gum, and six vitamin tablets (1942 versions had eight Charms and two packages of gum). It provided six man-days of (albeit meagre) rations when consumed with at least one pint of water daily. It replaced (2f) as standard life raft rations in 1942. (*2d*) *AN-W-5 emergency drinking water*, with a distinctly metallic taste, was supplied in 11 oz. cans with a screw cap. Early raft stocks had seven cans, but only one can was supplied when the JJ-1 and LL-1 desalting kits became available in 1944. Cans were also included in many of the E-series

emergency kits. (*2e*) The *type JJ-1 sea water desalting kit* contained six chemical briquettes and a vinylite bag. One briquette, mashed up in the bag, would desalt a pint of water. (The LL-1 kit was a much larger solar still assembly.) (*2f*) The infamous 1941 *type K field ration* consisted of three meals, each contained in an outer pasteboard carton and an inner waxed box (early cartons were colour-coded in a 'camouflage' pattern, but from 1943 most were natural pasteboard). This was the standard combat ration for all branches throughout the war. A meal contained two small, key-opened cans of various meat products and cheese spread; various combinations of ready-to-eat cereal, chocolate, and fruit (could be boiled to make a jam) bars; hard and soft crackers; packets of soluble coffee, sugar, lemonade powder, chewing gum, dextrose tablets, and bouillon cubes. Toilet paper, four cigarettes, book matches, salt tablets, and a tiny wooden spoon were also provided. K rations were a component of parachute emergency kits, until replaced by (2g)—K's provoked thirst—and many of the E-series emergency kits. An E-6 (rations) emergency kit (individual bail-out) is displayed; the E-7 (water) bail-out kit was identical. (*2g*) The *emergency parachute ration* was adopted in 1943 to provide a more compact alternative to K-rations, replacing them in emergency parachute kits and also found in the C-1 flyer's emergency vest. The can held two bouillon cubes, cheese and cracker bar, Charms candy, six pieces chewing gum, two chocolate bars, two packets soluble coffee, two sugar tablets, 15 halazone tablets, and four cigarettes. A 'P-38' can opener was taped to the can. (*2h*) The *air crew lunch*, adopted in 1944, held two fudge bars, two sticks chewing gum, and 2 oz. hard candies. These were contained in a pocket-size, two-compartment pasteboard carton with a sliding cover allowing its contents to be dispensed with one hand. It was issued on the basis of one per man on missions of more than three hours duration. On missions longer than six hours, crews were supplied with full meals of sandwiches (Spam being 'immensely popular'), snacks, canned fruits and juices, and hot soups and beverages.

L: Hell at 25,000 feet

Ideally, a disabled aircraft requiring the crew to bail out was set on a level course and slowed down. The realities of bail-out from a battle-damaged aircraft were far different, however. When spinning out of control, the resulting G-forces, often coupled with fire and airframe break-up, made bailing out a perilous and often impossible ordeal, with few surviving airmen admitting recalling details. The

A C-2 one-man parachute raft with its component MX-137/A radar reflector erected. The raft is orange-yellow with a medium blue spray shield fitted.

The crew of the 'Memphis Belle', 324th Bombardment Squadron, after completing its much publicised 25th mission in May 1943. This was the first crew to complete the required 25 missions (later increased to 30). The crew had amassed 51 decorations, but only the tail gunner received a Purple Heart. Unlike the motion picture of the same name, the 'Belle's' actual 25th mission was uneventful.

bail-out bell has rung, and these airmen struggle to make it out their designated emergency exits. These desperate young men wear alpaca-lined B-10/A-9 intermediate suits, with the exception of the right waist gunner (*L1*), who has retained his old B-6 'crusty' and is shedding his flak suit (M1 vest, M4 apron). His wounds treated, the contents of an aeronautic first aid kit litter the floor beside his M3 steel helmet. An electric heated muff has been slipped on his arm in an effort to protect it from the extreme cold. His mask hose is plugged into a low-pressure demand walk-around assembly. The left waist gunner (*L2*) rushes to snap on his A-4 QAC parachute. The .50-cal. M2 flexible machine guns, to protect the B-17E from lateral attack, are fitted with the old gun-mounted 200-round ammo containers; larger hull-mounted containers were introduced later. The radio operator (*L3*) armed with an A-17 carbon dioxide fire extinguisher, emerges from his fire-engulfed compartment wearing a B-8 back parachute. Already disconnected from the aircraft's oxygen system, he is activating his H-2 bail-out bottle. A discarded A-2 carbon tetrachloride fire extinguisher lies on the floor.

INDEX

(References to illustrations are shown in **bold**. Plates are prefixed 'pl.' with commentary locators in brackets.)

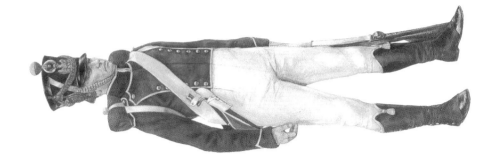

OSPREY
PUBLISHING

FIND OUT MORE ABOUT OSPREY

❏ Please send me the latest listing of Osprey's publications

❏ I would like to subscribe to Osprey's e-mail newsletter

Title/rank _____

Name _____

Address _____

_____

_____

Postcode/zip _____ state/country _____

e-mail _____

I am interested in:

❏ Ancient world
❏ Medieval world
❏ 16th century
❏ 17th century
❏ 18th century
❏ Napoleonic
❏ 19th century

❏ American Civil War
❏ World War I
❏ World War II
❏ Modern warfare
❏ Military aviation
❏ Naval warfare

Please send to:

USA & Canada:
Osprey Direct USA, c/o MBI Publishing, P.O. Box 1,
729 Prospect Avenue, Osceola, WI 54020

UK, Europe and rest of world:
Osprey Direct UK, P.O. Box 140, Wellingborough,
Northants, NN8 2FA, United Kingdom

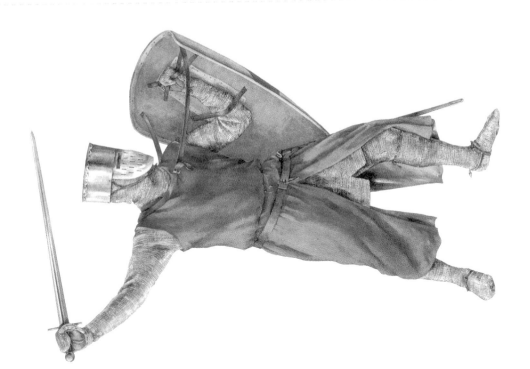

www.ospreypublishing.com

call our telephone hotline
for a free information pack

USA & Canada: 1-800-826-6600
UK, Europe and rest of world call:
+44 (0) 1933 443 863

Young Guardsman
Figure taken from *Warrior 22:*
Imperial Guardsman 1799–1815
Published by Osprey
Illustrated by Richard Hook

Knight, c.1190
Figure taken from *Warrior 1: Norman Knight 950 – 1204 AD*
Published by Osprey
Illustrated by Christa Hook

POSTCARD